DIGITAL SPINE

DIGITAL SPINE

A STUDY IN
BUSINESS STRATEGY

VIKRAM KALKAT & RETO GRUENENFELDER

Notion Press

Old No. 38, New No. 6
McNichols Road, Chetpet
Chennai - 600 031

First Published by Notion Press 2018
Copyright © Vikram Kalkat & Reto Gruenenfelder 2018
All Rights Reserved.

ISBN 978-1-64249-159-3

This book has been published with all reasonable efforts taken to make the material error-free after the consent of the authors. No part of this book shall be used, reproduced in any manner whatsoever without written permission from the authors, except in the case of brief quotations embodied in critical articles and reviews.

The Authors of this book are solely responsible and liable for its content including but not limited to the views, representations, descriptions, statements, information, opinions and references ["Content"]. The Content of this book shall not constitute or be construed or deemed to reflect the opinion or expression of the Publisher or Editor. Neither the Publisher nor Editor endorse or approve the Content of this book or guarantee the reliability, accuracy or completeness of the Content published herein and do not make any representations or warranties of any kind, express or implied, including but not limited to the implied warranties of merchantability, fitness for a particular purpose. The Publisher and Editor shall not be liable whatsoever for any errors, omissions, whether such errors or omissions result from negligence, accident, or any other cause or claims for loss or damages of any kind, including without limitation, indirect or consequential loss or damage arising out of use, inability to use, or about the reliability, accuracy or sufficiency of the information contained in this book.

Dedication

To our parents and families

Contents

Preface ix

Introduction 1

Classical Strategy Models Fail: Need for a Digital Model 5
    Blue Ocean & Red Ocean Strategy 7
    Reinventing Business Model 7

The Digital Spine Business Model 9
    Digital Rules 10
    Cyber Posture 13
    Global Economic Environment 14
    Organisation and Rewiring 16
    Social Demographics 18
    Business Value Chain 20

Digital Shift 23
    Impact on Economy 23
    Cybersecurity 26
    Blockchain 28
    Artificial Intelligence AI 30

Illustrations 39
    Uber 39
    Tesla 44
    Netflix 47
    Facebook 50
    Snapchat 53
    Amazon (Retail) vs. Walmart 54
    Apple 56
    Bitcoin & Other Crypto Currencies 60

    PayPal 64
    WeWork 66

New Markets 69
    Better Efficiency and Matching Quality 70
    Mobility 72
    Digital Momentum to Success: Seven Elements 75
    Learn to Work with Millennials 77
    Ageism Will Become More Evident 79

Conclusion 87
About the Authors 89

Preface

It took us only a couple of days to conclude that nothing in the existing business models actually worked nowadays. When we both started discussing the articles, the trends, the business cases faced by our Clients the obvious was quite evident. Anyone in business knew the digital theme coming up but it didn't simply stop there, the confusion of these rising young giants like Uber, Facebook, etc. continued to bring panic in conventional corporations. Even really large and successful software companies were panicking.

Restructuring had become a common theme and everywhere there were job losses and redundancies through 2016, and 2017. You couldn't find how you would survive in a few years and yet everything being transparent, the existing corporation at executive level were unable to comprehend cohesively, what was giving the oxygen and structure to all these new age companies? And one day while discussing this all we decided to start a discovery exercise by analysing it all ground up. We went through piece by piece through the interviews, the discussions, the failures of models and all our years of experience and put a new business model together. During these brainstorming sessions and reviewing and revisiting models and trends we saw the need for a more holistic model. We needed something that could singularly help explain these various questions, at the same time act as a drawing board for deeper and more complex strategies. And our journey took us to the Digital Spine.

Some of the pieces of the exercise were actually quite counter intuitive as not everything in the Digital Spine is simply about digital. There are pieces that are ranging from finance as the fall out from 2008 still runs deep in business world and has played a role in several areas of industry as well what people are willing to believe in. Furthermore, there are things that some might consider simple common sense but reality is rarely do these items get raised in strategic meetings and often no one wants to call them out. The theme around millennials was an important item that we brought forward in the book and think that this demographic trend is often ignored by most. Actually in the interviews we often noticed the generation gap in acceptance of cryptocurrency and other similar new trends. We discussed whether it made any sense to add figures, data and other similar details but then came to the conclusion to look at the future we have to discard the analysis of the past. Hence, the book in its current form and the way we pieced all together. We hope you enjoy reading it as much we did writing it.

Introduction

'Control your destiny or someone else will.'

– Jack Welch

How is it that a lot of knowledge and existing experience is no longer being considered a necessity in the success of these start-up models? Why it that sophisticated companies have been caught off guard by these new companies, unable to figure out whether these companies are truly threats until it's all too late?

We've written this book with a single purpose in mind, that is, to help existing corporations and young entrepreneurs who are looking for a holistic business strategy model to propel their businesses in the digital era. Companies and people are currently stuck with existing business models and strategies recommended in MBA schools and by management consultancies that have been around for a previous generation/era of environment. In the current landscape of digitisation, the requirements are different: there is a need for fresh ideas and approaches to compete.

We hope this book helps everyone better understand the key driving forces that make the new generation of companies more effective in business strategy despite lacking years of business experience, or lacking with regards to several business dimensional aspects (indeed, several of the existing business strategy models might have considered as 'barriers to entry' until a few years ago).

With the existence and elongated lifespan of Porter's business model, followed by Blue Ocean & Red Ocean Strategies, most of the sophisticated businesses have considered themselves well prepared for any strategic surprises to their existing businesses. Through availability of vast cash reserves for funding, most have bought advice the best of models, churned about analysis, and felt assured that their businesses are well protected from various scenarios.

But this has not been the case of late, as more and more industries and businesses have come to realise. Owing to digitisation, most leaders and even analysts haven't been able to recognise these new entrants. Most people (primarily from older generations) have found themselves quite sceptical about the success or their sustainability of the new breed of digital competitors. But with time a lot of the companies are having second thoughts as the true value and essence of the competitors haven't been correctly recognised using the existing business models. We believe the current business models in use are a core flaw in corporate strategy today.

We believe people need to unlearn several of the existing business models to better recognise the new one that we have introduced in this book. Further, we have taken the liberty of drawing comparisons among the high-profile companies that are best known in the business headlines nowadays.

While identifying new business models, it's important to recognise the process of themes to look for in the new breed of companies and the current digital landscape, recognise what sets apart the winners from the losers and know the process to check them over the days and months.

An important aspect that we came across during the selection of several illustrations and examples is the speed at which the economy and fortunes of these companies are shifting. These are all point of time analysis and as cybersecurity issues, leadership crisis, and other unforeseen items are coming to light it's putting several corporation in poor light at the same time.

The current environment has a substantial number of factors that either did not exist until a few years back or have matured a lot more only recently and led to the success of several of these companies.

People may come across some thoughts and ideas on digitisation in an intuitive manner. Our intention is to help bring to paper a process or an approach whereby the intuition, experience and insights of digitisation can be assembled to help people be better prepared for businesses ahead in this decade.

While reviewing these models, please note that there is an assumption that the environment for digitisation and stability already exists. This is important because, in situations of extreme economic or geopolitical crisis, the resulting disruptions of infrastructure and the normal working of the society might well wreak havoc with several of these models.

In this introductory chapter we highlight some key trends and themes before delving into details. The next few topics are to help give an understanding and perspective with regard to business themes.

Digitisation

Digitisation is a broad word that is often used in different contexts including automation, process improvements and other aspects. But the core of the digitisation concept is all about an entirely new end-to-end transformation that many businesses miss. We emphasise how digitisation in its true form is revolutionising businesses and industries.

In simple words, digitisation is the conversion of text into a digital format. But nowadays 'digitise' has become a verb that is loosely used across the industry to include the conversion of a variety of industries from conventional forms of business processes to use of internet-based tools and other, similar activities that didn't exist up until a few years ago. It is the use of 'digits,' or 1s and 0s in electronic or engineering terms, to find a new format and logic for existing business activity.

The popularity of digitisation is no fad, not an illusion that will fade away. It is based on an approach that shows extreme speeds, efficiencies of processes and, in some instances, entirely new business value chains that are unmatched using conventional or mechanical tools.

It has impacted all types of industries and now, more than anything, the way of life in most societies. With the advent of social media there are now sites that boast of more active users than the populations of the most populous countries of the world.

Industrial Revolutions and Industry 4.0:
A Current Digitisation Boom?

Previous industrial revolutions were all marked by increases in output and GDP. This Industry 4.0/digitisation boom[1] is marked by an increase in efficiency that has dramatically improved the way of life rather than raised the GDP. There has been a massive increase in data, including 'big data,' and a substantial increase and improvement in artificial intelligence and cognitive computing capacities.

---

[1] 'Industry 4.0 after the initial hype: Where manufacturers are finding value and how they can best capture it,' McKinsey report 2016

The current Industry 4.0 revolution might not be supported by a rise in the GDP of the USA and other developed countries, as in previous revolutions. It's therefore important to be clear on where the focus of the current progress is going to be, so that the focus of the new start-ups and strategy be reasonably aligned with those expectations. Governments and other institutions will be focusing their attention on activities related to these technological advances as they make regulations and allocate funding.

Millennials

An important change that will make itself more and more evident in the coming years is the addition of the millennial generation both as the prime consumers, employees, employers and inspiration leaders in the coming years and decades. This shift is an important one to better understand as this is the first generation that has primarily grown with a substantial portion of digital and information technology based devices all around them. The expectations of the possible is quite different for this generation unlike previous ones that were born and brought primarily in a mechanical world. How they perceive the future and what they consider as security, needs and wants will be different from versus what we witnessed in the previous several generations since the Great Wars. Millennial participation and expectations should be part of the overall strategy when looking at the digital future from all aspects.

Classical Strategy Models Fail: Need for a Digital Model

'Change is the law of life.'

– John F. Kennedy

Summary: *Porter, Blue & Red Ocean strategies and other similar popular strategic business models have been the bedrock of the industry for the past several decades despite the advent of the internet and other technological transformations. But unlike in previous decades, digitisation is an entirely new theme, as explained in the previous chapter; therefore, it is opening up deficiencies in the existing business models that are no longer able to provide holistic solutions to businesses. This chapter explains the gaps and why there is a need for a new business model.*

Porter's model (referred as Porter) requires and in some instances, **assumes that there is existing competition within the environment.** Porter does not visualize forces or models that might be outside the current environment. This would mean Porter is often unable to consider how technology is rapidly changing the landscape.[2]

In the age of digitisation, Internet of Things, and other advances, there has been a rapid convergence and evolution of new business models. Activities and topics that seemed to be outside the realm of a given business environment in previous years and generations now seem within reach. Digitisation and globalisation have abruptly brought to the forefront many ideas that would have been considered 'outside the box' solutions a few years back.

It also exposes some of the key issues in Porter's business model that **is useful for current industry analysis and existing**

---
[2] http://www.free-management-ebooks.com/faqst/porter-07.htm

competitors, but it is unable to tackle the speed and dynamics that globalisation and digitisation are together throwing in all parts of the marketplace.

With transfer of information, access to a much wider range of technology has made a lot of barriers to entry disappear, in the process disrupting traditional models that have been untouched for decades.

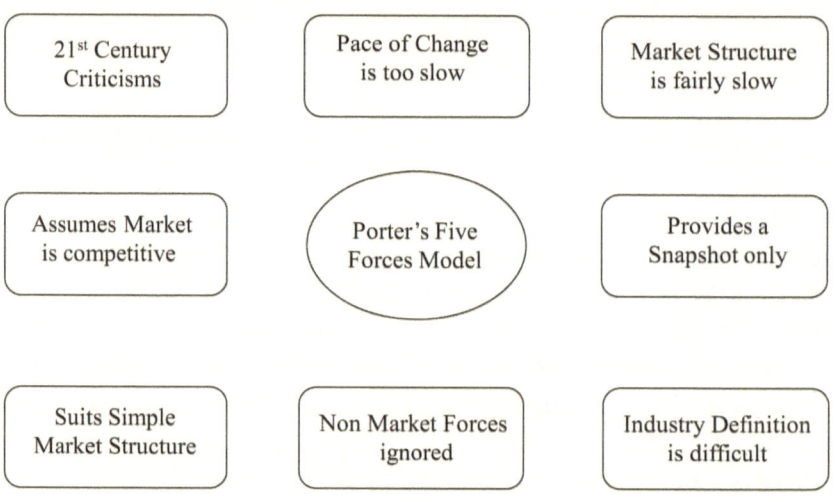

Figure 1: Porter's Model and Its Inherent Assumptions

For decades, a key success factor for some large corporations has been the barrier created by the experience curve. For years the motor industry has remained limited to a few large companies existing globally. The ones that rose up in niche markets continuously struggled to define their existence because of lack of sales or other complications in the manufacturing process that made them unable to compete. But these barriers and others were all blown away by Tesla, which has rapidly brought the automobile industry from its days as a loss-making industry built on decades-old internal combustion engine technology into the new age.

Tesla has managed to do this by using electric – and battery charging–based technology as its basis. This is one of several ways that are exposing deficiencies in existing classical strategy models.

Blue Ocean & Red Ocean Strategy

In Blue Ocean & Red Ocean Strategy, "the authors draw the attention of their readers towards the correlation of success stories across industries and the formulation of strategies that provide a solid base to create unconventional success – a strategy termed as "blue ocean strategy." Unlike the "red ocean strategy," the conventional approach to business of beating competition derived from the military organization, the "blue ocean strategy" tries to align innovation with utility, price and cost positions."[3]

This strategy[4] is made specifically to find solutions that are out of the box. But this business model strategy is unable to define a structured approach to be used in a digital environment. As the digital environment gets more established, there is a gap between existing Porter framework and the Blue Ocean approach that can help the executive management level to use a process-oriented, rigorous and structured approach to tackle organisational change and directional issues in the immediate environment.[5]

These considerations are:
- The pace of change is now more rapid.
- Market structures in the model were seen as relatively static.
- The model provides with only a snapshot of the current environment.
- It can be difficult to define the industry.
- The model does not consider non-market forces.
- The model is most applicable for analysis of simple market structures.
- The model is based on the idea of competition.

Reinventing Business Model

Johnson[6] et al. proposed that, in any business model, the essential strategy revolves around the concept of 'customer value proposition' (CVP).

---

[3] https://en.wikipedia.org/wiki/Blue_Ocean_Strategy
[4] http://www.free-management-ebooks.com/faqst/porter-07.htm#ixzz4p3tIizaP
[5] http://strategyatheinz.blogspot.in/2015/11/blue-ocean-strategy-limitations.html
[6] Mark W. Johnson, Clayton M. Christensen, Henning Kagermann, Reinventing your Business Model, Harvard Business Review 2008

This, in a nutshell, is made up of a few components and high-level formulas, which include:

    A. Revenue model: Price X volume;
    B. Cost structure: direct and indirect costs;
    C. Margin model: derived from revenue model and cost structure;
    D. Resource velocity: how fast we need to turn our inventory.

Several key features in this model have been exposed as deficiencies in the digital era. These include the revenue model, which is primarily dependent on volume. In the digital era, price and volume are no longer always linked. Resource velocity is dependent on inventory, but this is often not present in the new pure-digital companies.

Even though this reinvented proposal of a business model is not all that old, it shows how rapidly digital transformation is putting the thoughts and ideas that were considered revolutionary a few years back into question.

The Digital Spine Business Model

'Choose always the way that seems the best, however rough it may be; custom will soon render it easy and agreeable.'

– Pythagoras

Summary: In this chapter, we provide a new approach to digital business strategy. The digital disruption has not always focused on the latest technologies, but rather on different business models that are moving across conventional barriers of business understanding. We offer an explanation of a business model that helps weave across the various digital themes to help construct how the digital businesses are evolving and thriving.

There is a need for a holistic new business strategy model that helps better predict digital business patterns and disruptions better. Corporations are often only focused on improving a few sections of the business value chain and organisations with compensating for substantial gaps or missing elements across the overall digital model.

Porter's five forces, SWOT analysis, Blue Ocean strategy and the component business model have all been standard practices for decades, but they are unable to predict the rise and strategies of digital companies, i.e. the likes of Facebook, Tesla and Uber, amongst others. The digital disruption has not always focused on latest technologies but rather different business models that are moving across conventional barriers of business understanding.[7]

The need for a business model that fully embraces the digitisation of the economy has become obvious. The Digital Spine Model, which we have developed and present in this book, has digitisation at its core.

---

[7] https://www.cnbc.com/2017/05/16/the-2017-cnbc-disruptor-50-list-of-companies.html

10 | Digital Spine

This model is a synthesis of key speeches by leaders at global forums such as the World Economic Forum (WEF)[8] and publicly available reports from leading consulting firms. The Digital Spine helps to explain how digital disruption can be better harnessed as a transformation tool rather than a nemesis to existing businesses.

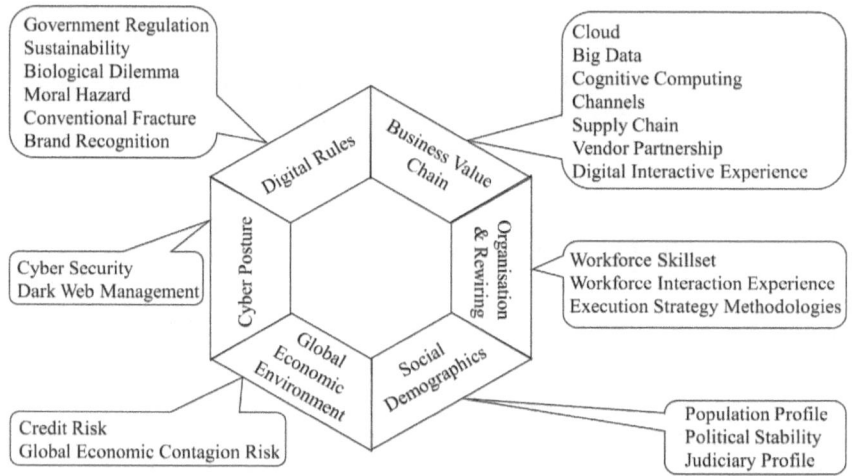

Figure 2: Digital Spine

Digital Rules

Government Regulations

Do the government regulations help or erode business strength? Does regulation create a new business ecosystem?

With the advent of global regulations and the influence of stronger super organisations such as OECD (Organisation of Economic Co-operation and Development), EU (European Union) and G8 (Group of Eight nations), there has been an increase in coordinated action by several countries at once. This means that government-based regulations can often be more effective than ever before in the history of mankind.

Further, with more educated governments and better information-gathering tools available centrally, governments are able to harness digital regulatory power more effectively than ever before.

---

[8] www.weforum.org

Net Neutrality is a critical digital rule that sets the playing field between large and small companies as well as service providers of internet infrastructure such as the telco and cable companies versus the pure internet based companies.

For the longest period net neutrality has been at the heart of internet world over. But as time passes several of the cable and telco companies have come under pressure of falling revenues and ability to upgrade infrastructure. There is a possibility that in coming years across the globe we might see more and more lobbying by companies to reconsider this.

Change in net neutrality has a direct impact on the business supply chain portion of the digital model amongst other aspects of the eco system.

Hence, several basic rules of information age that have long been taken for granted might be subtly changed by countries and will invariably lead to substantial changes amongst the digital business models.

Sustainability

Does sustainability provide enough business edge?

Sustainability of the finite elements in the environment, be they animals, forests, marine life, agriculture and so on, is now viewed quite differently with the advent of big data availability, sophisticated sensors, accurate satellite digital images, heat mapping, etc. How a decision on sustainability is made today is different from how it would have been even a decade ago, all owing to much more accurate count and feedback loop of information.

Biological Dilemma

Does digital technology provide an edge over existing processes and procedures for creation of biological creations? Does digital technology help or hinder existing life and environment? Is the digital disruption or innovation going to take it on the path of dilemma for any biological production?

Biology and life sciences might appear removed from digital influence, but the reality is that increasingly the results of a number of complex experiments are supported in both accuracy and sophistication with the availability of digital instruments. Further increases in this sophistication will influence how we imagine the chemistry lab of the future.

Moral Hazard

How does the business model impact moral questions? Can the business approach create moral dilemmas owing to its processes, information availability and other activities?

As the world becomes more interconnected digitally, it means we not can only influence people but also directly impact businesses, and hence livelihoods, in every neighbourhood across the globe. Is it always a positive impact? Are we always culturally correct to interpret what is meaningful? By what we accomplish with digital technology, be it delivery of software, a report, news, etc., how will the digital business model be used somewhere that we are simply virtually influencing (several corporations might be based in digitally advanced nation while the business model might be impacting adversely in a lesser developed nation owning to existing issues)? This is a moral hazard and dilemma that everyone needs to understand.

Conventional Fracture

Will the digital model accelerate the fracture of the conventional business models it plans to compete against?

Several business models seem to work until they are literally broken by a 'killer app' or an internet-based business model that brings about efficiencies beyond reach. Whether the use of the digital approach supports or accelerates the demise of an existing conventional model is a critical economic item to review. Often the expectations are much higher than usual, owing to excitement of the new digital approach, but only when all the process and regulations are studied can the frictional cost be calculated.

Brand Recognition

How is the brand impacted by the digital edge? How is the brand perceived in the digital environment vis-à-vis the existing business? What is the marketing impact across generations? Is the brand considered 'cool' amongst the millennials?

Nokia was one of the most recognised brands, and yet within a brief span of time it was overtaken by Apple in the mobile marketplace. Nokia was considered by many to be an older-generation phone, while Apple was considered 'cool' by the millennials. The demise was extremely rapid. Brands are made and lost very quickly, and in the digital era even more so. Brands, both in the conventional and even more in the virtual environment, play an exceptionally important role. The manner in which the brand is perceived can substantially impact business.

Cyber Posture

Cyber Security

How is cyber security graded in comparison to existing benchmark and global business levels? In the digital world as in our physical world, we need to address security.

In the digital era where security is virtual, data in most cases is the primary asset of the companies. Cybersecurity is thus considered a bedrock requirement for all companies.

Cyber Security is expected as a baseline for all digital strategy models; therefore, a lot of emphasis is required to ensure this is always at par with high standards and trends. With increase of cyber incidents globally and with hackers able to penetrate from anywhere, it's quite hard to stay ahead of the game in this, and this requires a lot of planning and understanding to ensure that it is correctly set up.

Cyber security will not only impact information technology but also Operation technology. As there is an increasing convergence of virtual and physical worlds, owning to Internet of Things and Industrial Internet of Things based technologies, standards and protocols, we will witness a further convergence of the physical world devices such as cars, engineering equipment, home devices, etc. with the information technology world. This all will suddenly bring to the forefront an entirely new dimension of cyber security risk safety concern across the society world over.

Overall, there is a need to better understand the intricacies and boundaries of our digital environment so we can better protect our boundaries. Data leakage and other forms of virtual threats will continue to haunt all companies; therefore, they always need to be ahead of the hackers and cyber criminals.

Dark Web Management

Are the business environment and the product impacted in any manner by 'dark web' and 'dark pool' activity?

Dark Web Management is about forums that are accessible on the world wide web through special software, and hence they are hidden from the public domain. Dark Pool Management is regards to financial securities in private exchanges. Both the activities are considered synonymous with criminal activities. Considering the increase in sophistication in 'dark web' and 'dark pool,' does the business need to take an active management role in monitoring or reporting on possible trends?

Global Economic Environment

Credit Risk

What is the credit rating as per the leading financial institutions (and credit rating agencies) for both the business and the industry?

Credit rating forms the basis of levelling the business financial risks across businesses, industries and countries globally. We are moving more and more into a world where we need to have a few quick gauges to help clarify the financial risk of investing in a business and the globally recognized credit rating agencies play an important role in this. Fitch, S&P and Moody's remain the most recognizable names in credit ratings and assessments. An uplift or a decrease in ratings by these agencies almost certainly creates ripples for the business.

During a crisis situation, as witnessed during the 2008 financial crisis, and soon afterwards during the debt crises of Greece and other countries, the rating agency downgrades can sometimes by themselves create a panic and a vicious cycle of its own. The downgrades and negative impact on the business unleashes market forces that are almost unstoppable.

Stability in the global economic environment via the rating agencies and other salient pillars is imperative for business stability.

These agencies ensure that a large business or a country tracks its overall financial and business decisions sensibly. The analysis of these agencies helps ensure that there is adequate financial sophistication to understand the overall economic environment of growth and depressions. But sometimes their decisions by themselves can create panics as well.

Global Economic Contagion Risk

What is the risk of a global economic contagion and its impact on the business?

Global economic contagion is the spread of financial and economic crisis across the world. It is caused by sudden and dramatic movement of financial markets followed by an economic crisis or the collapse of a country's economy. Via the common threads of global trade, it is spread rapidly across countries and continents. Since, in today's world, the supply chains from manufacturer to end customer are all spread across the world, such a crisis can be felt even in the most isolated places.

For example, during the 2008 crisis as prices of items such as woollen clothes dropped, it resulted in a drop in the price of the expensive pashmina, which is extracted from goats. This, in turn, resulted in a crisis in Mongolia, a place most would have considered well isolated from the economies of the west.

There are some key questions that need to be asked by companies that plan to expand in the digital world:

Can the business survive or benefit from a contagion scenario?

Would a global economic contagion provide more weightage to the digital model or instead erode its importance? (In extreme situations, would people flock to this business model vs. the existing conventional options?)

Global contagions, 'Black Swan'[9] events, and similar market crises are becoming quite common nowadays as the economic cycles become shorter and the world becomes more and more interconnected. Each time there is such a crisis, it often evaporates funding money, and often consumers freeze their spending even it's for a short duration and other similar issues that have negative consequences of the business.

---

[9] Nasim Nicholas Taleb, *The Black Swan: The Impact of the Highly Probable* (New York: Random House, 2010)

We need to ensure there is a stress test possible to figure out how much of such a crisis, and for what duration, the business can withstand.

Organisation and Rewiring

'Don't blame people for disappointing you. Blame yourself for expecting too much from them.'

— Buddha

Workforce Skillsets

How are the training, the skillset changes, and other activities around the workforce managed to adapt to the digital change? Will the current workforce adapt or be refreshed?

The biggest challenge faced in digitisation is having correct skillsets. Most people in management and executive roles who have directional responsibilities are well away from the age of getting reskilled or retrained. Many if not all of them have been trained in degrees that would be invalid in today's world because of so many rapid changes: MBA degrees from programs that taught now-outdated business models, engineering degrees that trained in technologies now becoming obsolete, and so on. In this age of rapid transformation, the skillsets required may well be those that have only been developed in the last few years.

Workforce Interaction Experience

Considering the changes in the digital environment within the organization and with external clients, how is the digital experience delivering better value?

The workforce of the future is expected to require a different set of skills. Also, the manner of work and culture is expected to be subtly different from today. Tools that will be pervasive in the future workforce, are going to be more in line with what we are observing being used by today's millennials. The communication response times, work timings, etc. will be adapting to new-age needs. This will mean that companies that adapt this interaction experience quickly are going to have an edge in attracting new talent and thus showing higher productivity in this new digital age.

But this not a simple task. This requires deep understanding of new skillsets and how they will be managed. This will mean that typical organizational verticals long considered standard in operations might now look different. With a dearth in new skillsets, how do you balance between investing in new talent and keeping existing employees who might feel insecure that their roles and jobs might be threatened in the next few years.

One of the key themes for the future will be that which centres around the collaborative environment. Here, the young and innovative will look for spaces to work where they can connect and collaborate in a harmonious manner. This environment will no longer be stifled by top-down direction and the drilled processes that were so prevalent in previous workforce setups. Rather, the workforce can be huddled around, working on a problem and feeling attached to a sense of mission.

Some key questions to ponder include:
1. Is the workforce feeling more empowered, or is it creating obstacles?
2. Are the external clients able to interact better with the workforce or is it creating confusion? What percentage of the workforce is made of millennials?
3. Is the company a place of choice for millennials to work?
4. Does the workplace environment promote a culture of genuine innovation and progress?
5. Do you have accurate data on how temperature, sound and other workspace details impact the focus and overall mind-set of the employees?
6. With work taking more of a 'co-working' approach, how is the current setup considered?

Execution Strategy Methodologies

How will change management adapt to the digital approach to business?

All strategies are ultimately tested during the execution. It is essential a lot of thought is given to the manner in which the strategy will be executed. The first step in the execution will be to understand that this is a task of change management. As the strategy is new, it will need to be championed and sold to the entire organization successfully before any execution commences. Once the change management is clearly articulated, it can be executed using a conventional programme management approach called 'design thinking'[10] if deemed necessary.

Key questions to ponder are:
1. Are the strategy and concept well understood by the organisation?
2. How will the organization execute the transition from a conventional approach to a purely digital approach?
3. Has the execution approach been used successfully before?
4. What are the underlying principles and methodologies behind the execution?

Social Demographics

'Technology is spurring innovation and the "demographic dividend" has brought change.'

– Nouriel Roubini

Population Profile

What is the population that can adapt to the digital change? Can the older generation adapt to the digital changes? What is the market size of the population that will adapt or successfully use the digital approach?

In any business strategy, the social demographic plays a key role. The future of any nation is its young population. The millennials will play a pivotal role in the future of most businesses, both as workers and as consumers. Therefore, the size of the younger generation, their education and exposure to digitisation will play an important role. The perceptions of the young population will help shape what is acceptable and attractive to them as forms of convenience, aspirations and imagination to allow businesses to help shape their strategy.

Already in a number of developed countries, millennials are becoming the largest number of employees. Hence, from the

---
[10] https://en.wikipedia.org/wiki/Design_thinking

employees' perspectives, a large portion of employees will demand newer approaches to organisation and processes and hence shape the culture of the organisations. Hence, it is urgent that a new business model be adopted rather than incurring the confusion that comes with using outdated ones.

Political Stability

How stable is the political system of the country to adapt to the digital changes? Will there be political interference with the new digital rollouts? Is there a massive change in the political environment, or will it cause disruption in the electoral mix that can have an impact?

For any business the regulatory environment is critical. This in itself depends substantially on the political stability of the country. In countries where political stability isn't guaranteed, it is hard for businesses to invest or flourish. Businesses will be hesitant to put down roots or expand as they are uncertain of how the leadership would perceive them and if there would be obstacles created. This is one of the core reasons that third world countries with poor political structures have struggled to entice the young generation to go into start-ups or seek venture funding to start new businesses.

Judiciary Profile

How sophisticated is the judicial system for ruling in digital-related legal disputes? Are the laws of the territory able to adapt to the digital changes?

In the new generation of business models, several of them will challenge the existing businesses. Sometimes the existing businesses will want to create obstacles by challenging the new businesses in courtroom battles. If business start-ups challenge existing trade unions or union-based rules that too can lead to strikes and complaints to the judiciary. This all means that countries that can provide fair, unbiased judiciaries may be the first to help start-ups move forward. Quick and balanced decisions from the judiciary are most supportive for start-ups and businesses. In the digital arena, where business models need to evolve rapidly, the judiciary of a country can play a critical role. As many of the businesses are asset-light, challenging businesses with out-of-the-box business models can often be perceived as a threat to existing businesses.

Business Value Chain

With the emergence of the internet twenty years ago, the exchange of data started, first amongst departments within the same corporation and later across industries. Years later, trust in the exchange of digital content was established and the adoption of open standards allowed the exchange of data across various vendor platforms. However, the software license fees of the big tech companies such as IBM, Microsoft and Oracle were excessive and prevented further progress in digitisation, until the software of open source[11] was established and trusted by companies.

Cloud

Open source became well established, providing operation systems (primarily Linux), various databases and programming languages. In addition, efficient cheap hardware (cloud), enabling the digital transformation at its full scale became available for an affordable price. This technology push allows sharing compute resources in the cloud, makes all kind of data available to anyone and provides a considerable economy of scale to corporations and private entities. However, the achieved interconnectedness requires new measures regarding privacy and security (cybersecurity) for protecting data. Technologies such as DevOps, which are built in the cloud, allow for instantaneous deployment of new applications, allowing companies to respond very fast to market change, competitive attacks, etc. This allows companies to realise competitive advantage. However, cybersecurity has to be very stringent, otherwise the enterprise might easily be jeopardized via cyberattacks.

Big Data

For the last few years, the amount of data has grown exponentially, about tenfold in two years. The majority of these data are publicly available, either through active sharing or as traces from digital activity,

---

[11] https://opensource.org/

e.g. via social media and mobile activity. These data do not have a particular structure, whereas private data, e.g. corporation-specific and relevant data do have a structure. The recent paradigm shift towards data democracy, meaning having more data, both structured and unstructured, available at much greater magnitude, opened new doors for the digitisation of the world. Big Data became the collective name of this new vast amount of data and its processing. Every day more and more data are moved from legacy infrastructure into the cloud. At the same time, the cloud applications themselves generate vast additional amounts of data daily.

Artificial Intelligence (AI)

The availability of all these data allows for gain new insights via the methods and approaches of Artificial Intelligence, which is the new idiom to summarise the algorithms of the traditional artificial intelligence, machine learning, neural networks, deep learning, cognitive computing etc. into one. A gigantic amount of compute power is needed in order to provide insights from these data. 'Remark: There is no AI without vast amount of data.' The competitive environment requires instantaneous insight for making accurate decisions on the spot. The computing power is provided by the cloud and is accessible via any channel. This opens to established companies and start-ups an entirely new world of innovation, service offerings, products, etc. AI is a key driver in the digital world and therefore a main contributor to the digital shift which is more elaborate in the next chapter.

Channels

Today, the primary access channel used for any service in the cloud is mobile devices. Most have a preliminary built-in additional sensor functionality and are therefore part of the Internet of Things (IoT). With the progress in voice recognition and movement recognition due to the advances in AI, a wider and richer range of data is generated. They are an additional data source from which insight might be deduced.

Supply Chain

The change in technology made markets transparent, and therefore the entire supply chain has changed from supply relationships that have been built and established over many years to 'who can deliver what I need now.' A prominent example is the disruption of the taxi industry by Uber. The change in the supply chain affects vendor partnerships. The classical sales person or client representative gets replaced.

Vendor Partnership

With the advancements in digital disruption, most particularly AI, the salesperson simply does not make any sense. All his explanations and discount models have no more relevance. The design-driven culture[12] relies on design thinking and fast prototyping to give a feel of what the new product or service delivers. It is easily customizable to the specific need. Achieving a goal does not depend on a single vendor. The compatibility between components and software modules allows to pick and choose from a range of vendors that work in collaboration to achieve a better and cheaper result faster. Visions and putting them into action are the foundations of disruptions, as demonstrated in the chapter illustrations.

Digital Interactive Experience (iX)

Interactive experience (iX) is almost the gateway to digital world. It is at the heart of any and all digital companies and strategies, playing a pivotal role. Interactive experience not only for the customers but also for the internal users is the key to success. Most successful digital companies such as Amazon, Apple, Google, Facebook and Snapchat have a simple, highly focused and yet unique interactive experience that glues its users and employees together.

Key questions to ask are:
1. Is the iX experience amongst the best three in its industry?
2. Is it simple and focused?
3. Would this be one of the core features of the company's digital strategy?

---

[12] http://www.mckinsey.com/business-functions/marketing-and-sales/our-insights/building-a-design-driven-culture

Digital Shift

As mentioned in previous chapters the need for replacing the conventional strategies and business models developed in the previous decades, we believe that with generations of MBAs and others trained across the globe in those strategic models will continue view several new digital innovations and breakthrough using the coloured lenses of strategies developed decades ago. This would mean they would inevitably come to inaccurate conclusions. There is a need to better understand some of these key elements or important building blocks in the digital world in the coming years.

The digital shift is inevitable, but with wearing the myopic lenses of strategies from previous decades many who hold important institutional and influential positions risk getting it wrong hence creating disastrous consequences for masses.

Impact on Economy

Summary: The next era of digitisation will impact all sectors in the economy, governments and the society overall through much higher levels of automation and the introduction of Artificial Intelligence. The automation activities, processes, will have a deep impact both on urban and rural societies. Our approach to gather information, building blocks of all sorts will be reassembled. In the immediate future, companies will have to attend to these business impacts by addressing organisation changes, process changes and overall acceptance of this new trend. As we are trying to address through the Digital Spine the existing business models will be redrafted.

Over the last two decades the internet and related technologies such as databases have revolutionized the economy by making the processing and exchange of data much easier. The push for open source over the last decade made cheaper IT available for everyone. Together with the recent explosion of data, due to available newer technologies such as cloud and cheaper compute power, a new era of digitisation for the economy, governments and the society overall takes place. Further as addressed further down in the chapter Artificial Intelligence will create an entire new shift on how information is gathered and automation is made substantially more efficient. During this era there is a tremendous change towards better, faster and cheaper solutions allowing to cut cost significantly.

The combination of Information Technology and Operation Technology improvements together will support a substantial increase in GDP, productivity and several other economic measures for developed countries. The current business value chain will all get refreshed hence services and manufacturing both will be see a new generation of efficiency like never witnessed since start of industrial revolution in early 19th century. Some ends of economy will have a positive impact while on other ends there will be negative impacts (owning to job losses). Overall societies will all go through deep changes.

Overall economies will see a substantial boost world over like never seen since the start of industrial revolution.

Automation of Process

With machines based on much higher levels of automation, this requires far fewer manual activities to be managed. The precision of work is much higher, and the number of control points to better understand the end-to-end generation process is better controlled with several automated alerts. As we move farther along into the era of artificial intelligence, several machines might even have the capacity to handle changes based on alerts and ranges set up. In essence, that's when they will have truly become immersed in digitisation.

Digitisation means overall higher fuel efficiency, optimized management and fewer breakdowns and requirements for spares. Furthermore, the use of AI has increased the ability to handle much higher levels of complexity in a supply chain while at the same finding new ways to reduce costs. This makes the emergence of automation across the globe a phenomenon that is definitely here to stay.

Trading

A key plus-point of digitisation is easier access to information. Information is more readily available, searchable and therefore accessed by many more people than just a few decades ago. Over time, the information-user interface to access the information has improved dramatically. Trading and related activities have seen a huge change from decisions being made based on this information. Furthermore, digitisation has allowed for much better tools of analysis, some directly owing to digital formats that can help with these, and others, simply as time has gone by, to the use of much better processors and powerful machines and the availability of new cognitive tools. Overall, it has improved decision-making and made for a better balance of energy and utility products.

Distribution

As we move down the chain to distribution, this is impacted by the vastly superior digital tools and information available. This supports fewer losses, higher workforce productivity and preventive maintenance. Distribution avenues will open to a much wider range as more sophisticated tools become available to analyse data at a much higher level of efficiency without increasing costs. Use of big data and artificial intelligence will both play a pivotal role.

Retail

The retail sector, owing to digitisation, has almost seen a revolution. With a much better supply chain and all the efficiency achieved in stages before, this has meant that retail has more accurate information, a wider range of selections, and better access to information for clients through simple yet sophisticated user interfaces. Tools available for both end users and others to make choices have grown dramatically over the years. Overall these include: individual new products, better prices and digital operations.

Group Headquarters

Optimised operations via better available management tools, data management, communication made simpler and cost-effective, better analytical tools to support management decisions (cognitive) and much more are being experimented with and added to help organisations become much nimbler.

Cybersecurity

Summary: Cybersecurity is a major concern in the digital environment. Cyber attacks jeopardise the enterprise. Security is a discipline and becomes a competitive advantage in the digital era. There are well known procedures and methods available helping to reduce the risk of security vulnerabilities. Cybersecurity is a concern beyond information technology, as with the expansion of internet of things and industrial internet of things the operation technology based devices will also require a deeper focus on cybersecurity issues.

The question about security always occurs when computing, storing and exchange of data is involved. The goals of security are confidentiality, integrity and availability. The threats to security are interception, interruption, modification and fabrication. A wide range of controls, such as encryption, programming controls, operating systems, network controls, administrative controls laws and ethical conducts are available to address these threats.

As the role of digitisation expands across into operation technology, with the next generation of engineering equipment that is more automated and better adapted to Industry 4.0 requirements, the need and concern for cyber security will expand. Cybersecurity for critical infrastructure, self driving cars, internet of things, and industrial internet of things based devices will become evident. This will force companies, and countries to re-evaluate their cyber posture beyond information technology.

Today security is commonly referred as cybersecurity to express the security in the cyberspace. With the progress of digitisation, issues with cybersecurity become more and more prominent.[13] Over the last few years cyber attacks become more known as with the internet it is barely possible to hide such attacks. The world became also more vulnerable towards cyber attacks as more and more data are stored in the cloud.

A significant root of the security problem is the lack of discipline of organisations and private users. The cybersecurity technology per-se

---

[13] https://economictimes.indiatimes.com/tech/ites/from-apple-to-uber-heres-a-list-of-massive-hacking-scandals-that-rocked-the-world-in-the-past/articleshow/61757429.cms

is safe, however its use asks for some discipline, there is no shortcut. The problem of security goes beyond technical and discipline aspects only as any attack has a direct impact on economics and privacy. Furthermore, human aspects play an essential role.[14]

It is evident that a perfectly working cybersecurity is a core pillar for any digital progress. Digital spine is based on the assumption that cybersecurity is already available at a high and sophisticated level. Cybersecurity in the digital era requires the same degree of vigilance for the health, safety and security of digital data as is understood to be needed in the physical world.

For most companies, cybersecurity would not act as a competitive advantage as the expectation would be for a high bar in all cases. What will become evident very quickly is that, if a data-based company isn't able to provide strong cyber protection or is exposed to cyber attack, this will lead instantaneously to a downward risk to the brand and an overall risk for legal and other loss-related issues. Cybersecurity for operation technology layer will not only require focus in terms of technology it also needs to be assessed from perspective of risk, operations perspective as well. Its will require focus beyond the CIO, and will possibly need to be addressed by the COO and CFO instead. There has been an increase in awareness of the exposure to existing critical infrastructure layers (of operation technology such as: Power, Water, Nuclear, and critical manufacturing industries). This will be an expanding cybersecurity domain in the coming years as next generation of machinery is introduced that's connected to Cloud and the internet in coming years.

There are thousands of examples illustrating the negative impact of the lack of rigorous security. The recent Equifax incident is just one off. Equifax's business model is built around storing credit checking and analysis information of millions of customers from USA and a few other countries. A simple patch issue exposed the data of hundreds of millions of customers from across the world over a period of two months. The manner of the cyberattack and the complete lack of professional response means the company will be exposed to several hundred class action lawsuits as well as some federal investigations and enquiries.[15]

The upside of not having a cyberattack is not having the issue at all. Therefore, in the digital spine model, cybersecurity should be taken as

---

[14] https://hbr.org/insight-center/getting-cybersecurity-right
[15] https://www.wired.com/story/equifax-breach-no-excuse/

a given in all cases, as with this weakness the rest of the digital spine becomes meaningless.

The risk of security threats in the cyberspace may be considerable reduced by:
1. Defining security as a process;
2. Defining, implementing and maintaining a rigorous up-to-date security architecture;
3. Enforcing 100% compliance with all security procedures;
4. Conducting regular security compliance reviews for all employees including the C-level;
5. Evaluating security holes and vulnerabilities through ethical hacking.

Blockchain

Summary: Blockchain as a theme will touch upon almost all types of global trade industries and more. This is, again, an evolving theme, how digital spine–based models are rapidly changing the conventional models and will show the path for revolutionary new approaches to business processes and change many existing business models.

Blockchain is a continuously growing list of digital records, called blocks, which are secured using state-of-the-art cryptography. Each block has a timestamp. The blocks are linked together and form the Blockchain, which serves as an open distributed ledger.[16] A block can contain any form of digital content. This open ledger may be imagined as a giant distributed database, as a tremendous spreadsheet, that runs on public computers distributed over the planet. This distributed computing is achieved thanks to the fact that all blocks and links are secured via cryptographic procedures. Furthermore, the distribution allows taking advantage from any compute resource that is made available. Therefore, enterprises which have already adopted the Blockchain technology, run it in the cloud. The required compute power grows daily.

Blockchain was invented at the end of the last decade in the context of the first cryptocurrency Bitcoin. The mining of cryptocurrencies relies on Blockchain and its compute power is provided by the so-called miners.

---
[16] https://en.wikipedia.org/wiki/Blockchain

The distributed ledger based on Blockchain opens a wide array of business opportunities in all industries that use digitisation and therefore will revolutionise the world.[17]

The core values for businesses of the digital distributed ledger Blockchain are its availability amongst peers who are interacting and the transparency to all its users without the need for third parties for verification;

Particularly international trade and commerce, the financial services sector and a wide range of industries that require ledger maintenance benefit from the use of Blockchain. In a financial context mostly private Blockchains are applied as this provides the operator the control who can read the ledger of verified transactions.[18]

As many as 19 distinct industries, ranging from banking to healthcare to shipping and a whole range of verticals, have been identified as having use for a common ledger that is untampered and can provide an audit and compliance trail for all those using it for partnerships and collaborations. Blockchain helps bring in multiple users who previously did not have access, owing to barriers to entry created by existing institutions or owing to strong risk/auditing features.

Blockchain can be analysed across the spectrum of digital dimensions, and it shows exceptional uses across several of the aspects within the business value chain.

iX Experience

Like most digital experiences, the interactive experience of a focused and simple approach that helps solve a very specific industry problem will be at the heart of its success. This ensures participation by consumers and enterprises globally. It can be anticipated that several different peer-to-peer technologies will compete and succeed or fail based on this.

In Blockchain there will be a wide range of usage of several other digital dimensions in the value chain, as noted below.

---

[17] https://www.mckinsey.com/industries/high-tech/our-insights/how-blockchains-could-change-the-world?cid=eml-web

[18] https://hbr.org/2017/03/how-safe-are-blockchains-it-depends

Supply Chain

The biggest impact in Blockchain technology is within the supply chain. All the users have access to the common ledger and have access at all times to the latest updates as well as the entire history. Legal and financial contracts could hence find much wider and more efficient methods to work with this.

Cyber Posture

At the core of Blockchain is its competitive advantage in cybersecurity. The security features of its architecture provide no requirement of third parties to assure authenticity. This helps bring in a large variety of users who were otherwise unable to be part of the system; furthermore, in terms of enterprises, it reduces the requirements of third parties. This will help revolutionise a lot of service-based activities and increase their efficiency.

If information can be sent and received between organisations that are safe, secure and auditable, this will support activities as sophisticated as contractual obligations. This will in turn make these activities much cheaper and also open up markets in countries and regions otherwise considered as having poor credit value.

Artificial Intelligence AI

Summary: AI is an important tool to gain insight from vast amounts of data. It is well suited to automate processes, advise professionals as medical doctors and lawyers. AI changes the way we work, makes many jobs redundant, makes cybersecurity stronger and similarly has substantial impact across a variety of professions and technology domains. AI requires new skills, such as the data scientist, apt in dealing with statistics and large amount of data.

The concept of AI has been developed according to Wikipedia in 1956[19] and was continuously refined since then. Today the term AI is commonly used for all sort of automated learning which can be achieved via a computer. Whenever human-like intelligence is artificially created the term AI is applied. In a nutshell AI is the application of a broad

---

[19] https://en.wikipedia.org/wiki/Artificial_intelligence

range of mathematical algorithms that process a vast amount of data to generate insight. Such insight typically is that the AI system takes a decision or provides to a human specialist meaningful insight such that she can take a more educated decision.

AI systems that take a decision or can make predictions are usually referred as machine learning. Typical examples are credit line approvals of a bank, system generated suggestions of the next movie you might want to watch or weather predictions. When humans interact with an AI systems to gain insight for support, the system is often referred as a cognitive system, e.g. it helps a medical doctor to decide on an appropriate treatment or supports a jury to return a verdict.

The mathematics behind all AI systems requires the availability of a vast amount of data. These data fulfil certain statistical properties which have to be known accurately. This insight allows the data scientist to decide which set of algorithms is best applied and according to which rules the data have to be prepared. In a next step the AI system is trained to provide accurate output. Once the pre-defined accuracy level is achieved the AI system becomes production ready.

The purpose of AI systems is to provide an answer in a very short period of time. Therefore, a gigantic amount of data must be processed in a very short period of time. To achieve that, cloud technology is commonly applied. Cloud vendors provide all required algorithms in the cloud. Therefore AI is today affordable and available for anybody that is connected to the internet, also medium and small enterprises. Many corporations however are still struggling with the application of AI as the correct use of data and algorithms often is a difficult task. This may be illustrated with the AI system based prediction of the S&P500 based on historic, e.g. not all companies that are listed in the S&P500 today have been listed in the S&P500 ten years ago, the S&P500 data itself are highly correlated, these data also depend on the bond market etc. With this example we would like to illustrate that when AI systems fail, it is not due to the system, it is due to the inaccurate preparation and/or use of data or inaccurate choice and/or application of an algorithm. The data scientist must have a solid knowledge of computer science, big data, statistics and algorithms. The domain/business expert is responsible for choosing the appropriate data sets which drive the business.

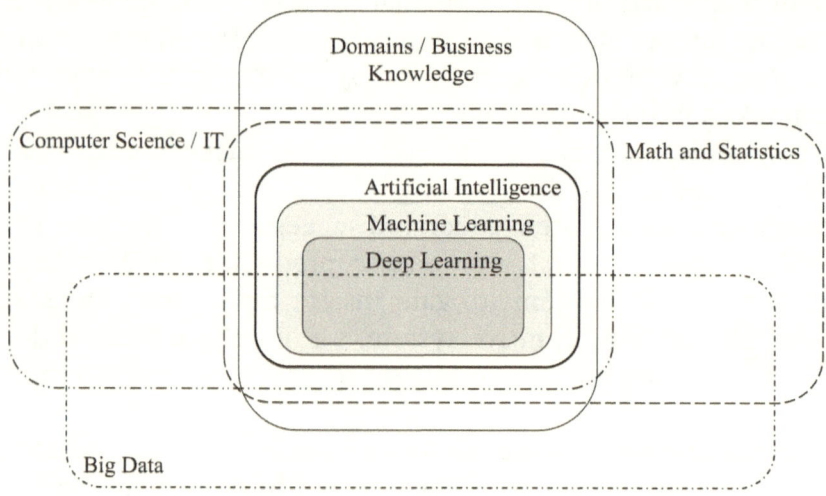

Figure 3: Context Diagram Artificial Intelligence AI

Usually data from most sources have to be cleaned prior to applying it to AI. This is particularly required when using unstructured data, e.g. sourced from social media or some Internet of Thing (IoT) devices. Pervasive computing, also known as ubiquitous computing, ensures that these IoT devices communicate properly between each other, perform useful tasks and make a best effort to deliver data as needed for AI.

Position of AI in the Enterprise

In these days, the success of most enterprises is still purely driven by its domain and business knowledge. Over the last few decades IT became an important support pillar and enterprises acknowledge its positive impact. Math & Statistics is in most enterprises either part of the Business (e.g. in the Financial Services Sector) or part of development in engineering companies.

The recent development and progress of Big Data and AI provides enterprises tools and methods to
- Gain a much deeper insight in their business;
- Automate tasks and jobs;
- Take better and more accurate decisions faster;
- Being more agile and responsive to market changes;

Embracing Big Data and AI shifts the current enterprise towards digitisation. To make this digital shift happen data scientists are needed.

This is a new profession that is specialized in all necessary matters of AI, computer science, statistics and Big Data. Universities already started to launch data science Master Degree programs.

AI Project in an Enterprise

Many enterprises already started in the recent years to apply AI technologies. New companies have been mostly successful as they were born into the digital age and did not have to deal with legacy. We illustrate the success of a few digital companies in the next chapter. In the past, established legacy companies often faced significant problems when applying AI. This is mostly due to the inappropriate use of data and the lack of skills which is today provided by the data scientist. To make an AI project successful at least the following questions have to be addressed.

Line of Business

1. What is the business objective of the AI project?
   What shall be automated?
2. Which facts and data are driving and impacting this business?
   Who inside and/or outside the enterprise can provide these data?

IT Department

3. Where to source the data?
   Which formats (structured and unstructured) have the data?
   What are the appropriate formats in which the data shall be represented?

Data Science Practice

4. What are the statistical properties of the data?
5. What kind of AI technology is most accurate to provide the objectives defined by the line of business?
6. Apply data to train AI.

Line of Business, IT Department and Data Science Practice

7. What is the quality of the training data based outcomes generated by AI?

Which changes are required to improve the accuracy of the outcomes for signing off the AI system as ready for production?

Warning: The successful application of AI requires some rigor. Unfortunately, still many managers believe that it is possible to simply apply a publicly available AI algorithm and to achieve quickly some great results. However, there is no short cut which prevents from unwanted surprises.

AI–Into the Mainstream/National Agenda

'Artificial intelligence would be the ultimate version of Google. The ultimate search engine that would understand everything on the web. It would understand exactly what you wanted, and it would give you the right thing. We are nowhere near doing that now. However, we can get incrementally closer to that, and that is basically what we work on'

– Larry Page

Summary: A new race not that might look much different to an arms race or a similar technology shift where there is competition across the globe. This new technology mania might have gone unnoticed in the last two years but soon it will be focus of C suites and governments across the globe. For the coming several years there will be a continuous upward trajectory of innovations, and focus across the globe similar to the dot com mania.

It is now common knowledge that super powers and developed countries at the highest levels of leadership are recognising AI as the future of technology, a line of defence and an overall competitive advantage of the nation.

Several countries are already willing to pour in billions of dollars into the efforts over the coming decade to be able to stay abreast against others.[20] Several political leaders have openly quoted that leaders in artificial intelligence could wield enormous monopolistic powers as well.[21]

Up until a few years ago these statements would have been considered as a bit far-fetched. But with recent game show victories on television by IBM Watson in "Jeopardy" game and Google's AI win over

---

[20] http://money.cnn.com/2017/07/21/technology/china-artificial-intelligence-future/index.html

[21] https://www.cnbc.com/2017/09/04/putin-leader-in-artificial-intelligence-will-rule-world.html

the "Go" champion have deeply impacted the vision of both leadership as well as mainstream public of what is imagination vs what is possible with the new breed of AI technology.[22] [23]

With saturation of several business models of software in business analytics, strong competition in cloud technology and outsourcing most large corporations are looking at new business fields to enter that can be potentially worth billions of dollars of investments and returns over the coming decades.

From that perspective AI has very well fit into that bracket for large enterprise investments. As typically large corporations take directional decisions and then move their entire marketing and business channels in that direction over coming several years, we should see this theme and trajectory to increase across large corporations globally.

AI – Business Disruption Through the New Age AI Companies

'The development of full artificial intelligence could spell the end of the human race. It would take off on its own, and re-design itself at an ever increasing rate. Humans, who are limited by slow biological evolution, couldn't compete, and would be superseded.'

– Stephan Hawking

Summary: AI technology is soon gaining critical mass in terms of investments, and innovations to be an essential part of business and commercial strategy of companies. This will mean a lot more commercial focus will be given to its uses and placement across large and small companies globally.

AI is a key element in the business value chain of the digital spine model as explained in the earlier chapters. As the technology via Cloud and other business models will allow investment to be broken down into smaller modules. The AI might not be a single large investment, but instead it will be a mix of several smaller modules.

---

[22] https://www.techrepublic.com/article/ibm-watson-the-inside-story-of-how-the-jeopardy-winning-supercomputer-was-born-and-what-it-wants-to-do-next/
[23] https://techcrunch.com/2016/03/15/google-ai-beats-go-world-champion-again-to-complete-historic-4-1-series-victory/

With the easier availability of Cloud based technologies software, hardware and AI related tools will be more easily available to smaller companies that can mix and match details to help package cost effective and innovative solutions to large enterprises and government institutions.

This is already leading to a substantial increase in AI related activities across several countries even in developing nations such as India.

Several billions of dollars' worth of investments has already been allocated to this new industry and more and more of the brightest engineers are graduating not to join salaried employment but rather to be entrepreneurs. Venture capital funding, angel investment are not only pouring in funding but also helping support with experienced management and channels of opportunity to help grow this industry at a rapid pace. The new investment and companies are well aware of the pitfalls of the dotcom era and as we have argued in the book above as long as they ensure they can follow directionally the digital spine based themes they can achieve business success.

This high intensity of investment, research and innovation is creating an entirely new technology and industry line of its own. Several large companies such as IBM are betting their future growth based on the pervasiveness of AI.

Several analytics companies have made fairly aggressive predictions not only about how AI will transform various industry verticals in the next decade, but also in the close future of the next few years. AI being a central piece in the Industry 4.0 related activities most analytics companies expect it to be centre of attention of C suite for several years to come.[24] [25] [26]

With the rise of the new age AI companies, some are expected to be bought over by larger enterprises (as it's already been happening in the past few years), while others may decide to continue independently and rise to become the next generation of leaders in the field.

---

[24] https://www.gartner.com/smarterwithgartner/top-trends-in-the-gartner-hype-cycle-for-emerging-technologies-2017/

[25] http://sea.pcmag.com/feature/17745/gartners-top-10-strategic-technology-trends-for-2018

[26] https://aibusiness.com/ai-market-growth-to-reach-47bn-in-2020/

Overall it offers a promising new future to the millennial generation both for employment opportunities and also ability to shape work culture and type of research to be funded for future. As the new AI companies will start with a fresh platform they might in the next decade be able to take up the goliaths across industry verticals.

The new generation of AI companies will rise much faster and with availability of better technology tools lower investment, cleaner and accurate data, will allow millennials to form better more mature AI based platforms and products at a rapid rate.

Future Employment

Summary: With availability of technology tools more easily available and better environment to launch start-ups the majority of millennial employment will come from small and medium scale companies. And several of these will rotate around AI as a technology or as a tool to harness other aspects that can be linked to it.

There is a flurry of thought around technology holding the future of job prospect because of the advent of AI. The rapid progress in cloud technologies provides to start-ups and established enterprises the easy and cheap access to a wide variety of AI. Many classical job tasks that ask for decisions or classification may be totally automated without any human interaction. This allows enterprises to obtain faster, better and cheaper outcomes. Even the IT industry will be impacted by e.g. automated code generation and built-in self-healing mechanisms in such a sophisticated manner that this won't require too many engineers, or others to service this technology.

Therefore, we foresee in agreement with the former Citibank CEO Vikram Pandit that a significant number of current jobs will disappear over years.[27] Society will have to face the challenge that there is less work available for the world population. Cost Income Ratios of companies will improve.

The future of employment might still be there in building a new generation of AI tools and also a new generation of designers. But both these skills might be a hybrid of how people are imagining today.

---

[27] http://fortune.com/2017/09/13/the-former-head-of-citigroup-says-30-of-bank-jobs-will-be-gone-in-five-years/

Moral Hazard

'With artificial intelligence we are summoning the demon. In all those stories where there's the guy with the pentagram and the holy water, it's like – yeah, he's sure he can control the demon. Doesn't work out,'

– **Elon Musk**

Summary: *A core feature in business strategy in digital era will be to consider moral hazard and issues as part core understanding of the overall issue, so that as the technology matures it's boundaries well thought through beforehand. This is an approach to technology like never thought before in previous technology shifts as now a lot of these new innovations might occur at a rather quick pace.*

'The real question is, when will we draft an artificial intelligence bill of rights? What will that consist of? And who will get to decide that?'

– **Gray Scott**

Ability to sift through data, allow for facial recognition and much deeper level of analysis at a rapid has become a source of attention both for government authorities and a key concern amongst the civil rights institutions across the globe. With the ability of do a variety of activities earlier though not possible either owning to sophistication of analysis or requiring rapid automation have are now going to be made available in the next few years. The key question is who will make the decisions on how to use and deploy these within a nation?

It might be no different than a sharp edge knife that can used both domestically or for a deadly sin.

Illustrations

'In this bright future you can't forget the past.'

– Bob Marley

This chapter provides some insight into how digitally disruptive companies have either been created from scratch or transformed themselves. All of the companies we look at cover parts of the Digital Spine Model as described previously. Collectively, the companies considered provide an exhaustive digital coverage leading to the Digital Spine strategy model.

Uber

Summary: Uber is a story of pure digitisation, where a company is able to harness the true potential of digitisation by correctly correlating the key elements of its business value chain, demographic appeal, organisation and rewiring correctly. With this and other successful execution steps, Uber has managed to catapult the brand globally in a record timeframe. But at the same time its rise has shown the questions and gaps that need to be addressed by the new age companies that can quickly bring it down. Those include, quality of workplace culture, and cybersecurity both of which are quiet easily ignored as they are not directly linked to revenue generation.

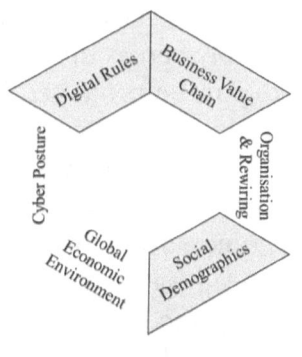

Business Value Chain: Supply Chain, Big Data management, Mobility, iX (user interaction)

Digital Rules: Government regulations

Social Demographics: Population profile

The Uber Story has multiple dimensions that have been analysed and re-analysed over the past several years. The dimension that interests us here is how it maps into the Digital Spine.

The various facets of strength exhibited by Uber show the Digital Spine as the centrepiece of its strategy. Uber is all about making the daily life of commuters more convenient and providing quality services at a cheaper price. As one spokesperson said in an online video, 'People will do what improves their quality of life. We give them their time back.'[28]

Uber has managed this quite innovatively by reusing assets already owned and available in an efficient and cost-effective manner. By ensuring that there is a vehicle available to the urban commuter within a few minutes of the click of button has brought service to everyone's doorstep as never known before. At the heart of it all is a splendid use of digital equipment, data and lots of other pieces that we will outline below.

Digital Rules

Uber has tackled the problem of government regulations that have often been the biggest hindrance for new entrants in the taxi service market, not only across the USA but also worldwide. Each city/municipality is likely to be protected by tight regulations that have been in place for decades. One surprising statistic often quoted is that the number of cabs permitted to operate in New York City at any one time has remained at approximately 60,000 since the early 1950s. And the situation had become so out of control that in recent years each taxi license has changed hands for as much as over a million USD! *Porter's business strategy model was unable to provide an answer to solve this problem.*

According to the conventional wisdom, absent any change in government regulation, this was an impossible situation. But there are always out-of-the-box solutions. In today's world, with the availability of digitisation, there are always linkages of extreme accuracy and high-quality, data-driven solutions to be brought forward.

Uber, through sheer grit, handled government regulation city by city. Its directors were able to manage this because of their ability to have a huge volume of assets and a high number of drivers available at their

---

[28] https://www.youtube.com/watch?v=pb–rJGgVIo

disposal, amongst whom several could easily help meet the requirements at any given moment. Furthermore, with the available of digital technology they made this all happen with a very lean organisation and without owning any assets themselves (e.g. the drivers owned the cars), therefore limiting their risk on capital at stake at any given time.

Uber has also sensationally claimed how, by reusing existing cars on the road, they are not only making urban transport sustainable but also helping reduce the carbon footprint and allowing cities to reclaim park spaces previously lost to parking lots.

Business Value Chain

At the heart of Uber is its ability to provide quality and efficient service at everyone's doorstep. This is made possible by the purely new business value chain tools that either were never available with conventional strategies or had constituted only a minor part of the overall feature for a long time.

High Quality Interactive Experience

The interactive experience starts with a very focused, easy-to-use interface. This has been well managed and is supported by lots of analytical tools to help give maximum relevant information to the user as well as a strong feedback loop to the Uber team for future use.

Uber uses big data, cloud and mobile technologies to ensure that its vehicles are available in urban areas within a few minutes of request. Handling this complexity with the precision that Uber has managed could only have been possible in the past in defence or high-end areas. But Uber has managed to arm its army of service providers with maps and high-quality communications information simply by using innovations of already-available technology.

Also, there are items that they have kept both its clients and its partners (drivers) hooked to the service, and that is its interactive experience. When someone orders a taxi and sees it on the map moving closer, it gives a different kind of feeling. People at those moments are often either in a hurry or nervously trying to get information on how far away the cab is. This interactive experience initially helped give Uber an edge over its competitors, and therefore helped it get a huge fan base across the globe.

By ensuring there is a feedback loop and information available online, Uber has been able to ensure not only quality but also flow of feedback, almost on an instant basis. Use of such digital technology now acts as a substantial competitive advantage over existing taxi service companies, at least in some instances. Further, it has allowed Uber to set up its global operations in a sustainable and scalable manner.

Vendor Partnership

Uber is now seen in many developed countries as a go-to place to get either a part-time job or, often in case of loss of regular employment, as a way to help fill in gaps. This has all been made possible by being able to work with simple contracts and a simple business model that allows for its army of drivers act as vendors who can easily and effectively work with this global company.

Advantage Social Demographics

Uber has catapulted very effectively on the social demographics as well. Urban societies the world over are becoming more and more uniform despite cultural differences. They are all full of younger commuters who urgently have to get to work on time and who struggle with rising costs of car maintenance, car parking issues and inadequate public transport. To add to all this, car and taxi services have been dominated by unions that have often been slow or apathetic toward hearing general consumers' voices, which have been getting louder and louder over the decades.

Targeting this young generation, which is armed with mobile phones, looking for good-quality service and more comfortable with online transactions and mobility-based applications, Uber has been an instant success.

In developing countries, Uber has been able to provide (after a few missteps) something that was never available to these countries in the past: a reliable service that could be tracked at all instances and drivers whose exact whereabouts could be tracked, available to local police and judiciaries whenever required. This made the services even more useful as it provided a sense of safety and security which was not available with the existing taxi services.

For many, there was miraculously available for the first time, a taxi service that was reasonably priced and gave a sense of safety and security. It was also a service that was available while on the move. Both the mobility and the safety factor made this an explosive success in countries such as India.

To top it all off is the leadership, the organisation execution skills at hand. Travis Kalanick (founder, and first CEO of Uber), as all those who have met him will agree, is a person with a vast amount of experience both in terms of handling start-ups and of having the grit to tackle a whole array of problems that typical start-ups come across. Having previous experience in successfully managing start-ups and also having the perseverance to work against extreme odds and powerful opponents, such as government regulators and unions across the globe, has been an exceptional tour de force for this young yet powerful global start-up.

His background helped him hire personnel and foster a work culture that has been exceptionally entrepreneurial, highly rewired for success as well as (what is often considered highly controversial) an aggressive impulse to compete.[29]

Overall, there was not a single factor that would ensure success or failure, but rather a full suite of new-age digital competitive edges that propelled Uber into a global success.

As time will tell, for those who want to compete against this new form of digital behemoth, there is an entirely new set of digital strategies and competitive advantages required that were unthought-of during the Porter Model era, and far more details than those envisaged by the Blue Ocean Strategy.

Cybersecurity Posture

'None of this should have happened I will not make excuses for it.'

– Dara Khosrowshahi,
Uber CEO, 2017

A recent development has been the exposure that Uber too has faced a cyberattack and the details of over fifty seven million users, and drivers was exposed in the attack. What was even more disturbing was how the entire incident was handled. Several activities regards to this are still under investigation, but overall its evident that the Cybersecurity posture even of such a sophisticated company is vulnerable. Cybersecurity gaps can very easily bring down the brand value of a company.[30]

---

[29] In 2017, Travis Kalanick was replaced by Dara Khosrowshahi owning to several controversies ranging from aggressive work culture to Government challenges across the globe

[30] https://www.bloomberg.com/news/articles/2017-11-21/uber-concealed-cyberattack-that-exposed-57-million-people-s-data

The manner in which a company tackles Cyberattack incidents more and more defines how the world perceives its culture for honesty and ethics and this will directly feed into its brand value for future.

Recently, exposure to several incidents has come to light with the change of leadership from Travis Kalanick to Dara Khosrowshahi. Uber will need to take several steps to improve that it's not only an innovative company where culture is to do "what works," but also be lot more transparent to ensure public safety issues, workplace culture issues, and similar activities are dealt with respect and speed.[31]

Tesla

Summary: Tesla is an illustration of a truly digital company that has taken several of the elements of the Digital Spine to help catapult itself to becoming one of the most powerful brands in an industry as complicated as the automobile sector. It's a perfect example of a company that might never have been conceived if viewed from the conventional business model lenses.

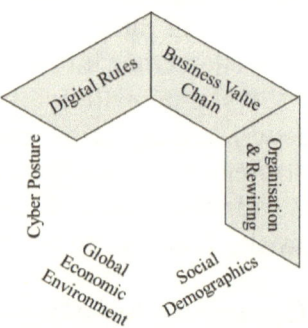

Business Value Chain: Supply Chain, Big Data management, Mobility, iX(user interaction)

Digital Rules: Government regulations, Sustainability

Organisation & Rewiring: Workforce skillsets, Workforce interaction and execution strategy

Unlike its competitors in the automobile sector, Tesla digressed substantially by becoming a purely electric car manufacturer. That, in a single stroke, took it straight into the world and strategy of a digital company whose competitive advantages would no longer be driven by Porter or other existing conventional strategy models of the automotive sector, but instead into an entirely new realm of competitive dimensions.

---

[31] https://www.bloomberg.com/view/articles/2017-11-22/uber-s-big-problem-is-a-culture-of-dishonesty

Its model ensured that it would fly past all government regulation, by not only being environmentally friendly but also by completely getting rid of the fuel combustion engine and all the related complexities and issues it caused by it. 'We have a giant fusion generator called the Sun,' its founder explained. 'It is already powering our ecosystem.'[32]

Many of its competitors have had to take a hard look at this while they grapple with the fines caused by diesel and petrol cars.

Business Value Chain

By starting from scratch, Tesla was also able to ensure that it completely changed the business value chain of the car. New paradigms appear:

'The drive to stop time should be around 20 minutes after every three hours...which what a normal person would do.'[33]

Comparing decisions made by a human driver versus a self driving car taking decisions per minute: 'It is like comparing how fast I run to the speed of light'[34]

By getting rid of the conventional engine with electric batteries, it was able to bring about a much larger space, ensuring new and cutting-edge designs and alloys for the car. It made the car much safer and more fuel-efficient, amongst other features that consumers were only able to dream of in the existing cars (even those at higher end of the spectrum).

One of the features all its buyers rave about is its highly wonderful gadgets, including a large-sized screen and other features that made the overall interactive experience give the 'wow' factor.

'Ludicrous mode' and mystique of sports cars...

Its move to digital has also ensured that, despite being a family car, Tesla is now often considered one of the fastest and safest cars on the road, taking up the mantle proudly kept for so long by the likes of Ferrari and other sports cars. This has been a huge blow to the entire sports car industry, which survived for a long time on the mystique of making cutting-edge cars that could go at fast speeds unavailable

---

[32] https://www.ted.com/talks/elon_musk_the_mind_behind_tesla_spacex_solarcity#t-421747

[33] https://www.ted.com/talks/elon_musk_the_mind_behind_tesla_spacex_solarcity#t-391246

[34] https://www.ted.com/talks/chris_urmson_how_a_driverless_car_sees_the_road#t-418965

in usual factory-made family sedans. Tesla's breaking of speed records against cars such as Lamborghini puts a huge question mark on the continued existence of these cars that are trying to compete using IC engines and other conventional approaches.

In a single lightning blow within a few years, Tesla has not only caught up with the best-quality brands but has set a new standard for automobiles across the world.

Vendor Partnership

At the heart of it all, Tesla has a unique vendor partnership. Unlike its competitors, by going electric it has brought in battery manufacturing to the heart of car manufacturing. The partnership of Panasonic, which has no experience in car industry, and Elon Musk, its dynamic founder (whose previous experience was in financial, internet and space technology) has brought a unique space age–like vendor relationship to the heart of the venture.

Organisation Rewiring and Skillsets

By solving the fuel combustion engine problem, Tesla has been able to attract an entirely new set of workforce people to the organisation. They are not like the previous generation's automobile workforce as seen in Detroit and other areas, but rather the best breed of engineers and designers competing to join the manufacturing plant. This leads to a fresh outlook on how the automobile industry is now being seen by others. Looking at the example of Tesla, many more Silicon Valley technology companies consider it possible to manufacture and compete in car industry like never before.

Elon Musk has been both a dynamic and maverick leader who, with his vast experience in start-ups and his financial muscle, has single-handedly changed one of the most complex of the conventional industries that most preferred to ignore. Furthermore, his unique outlook and vision have helped inspire and draw a lot of fresh and exceptional talent to the industry. This has been a huge edge for Tesla: without his background and vast experience it would have been a dubious venture lasting only a few years at the most.[35]

---

[35] http://panmore.com/tesla-motors-inc-organizational-culture-characteristics-analysis;

Social Demographic

The new breed of savvy urbanites (composed primarily of millennials) is ready to take up new technology with a lot more ease than previous generations. They are willing to take risks with the electric car chargers, scant as they are in some places, and to trade their existing hobby cars or even their prime cars for this new technology. They are much more eco-conscious and willing to support those who defy all odds.

California demographics and culture has as always been a huge support to the Tesla project, which has played well to the state's rebellious and innovative nature as it takes on the automobile giants. Also, in the current landscape with the global efforts against climate change, this growing movement across the world has also produced natural followers and supporters of Tesla.

Therefore, both the demographic factor and the 'moral hazard' caused by conventional fuel-based cars have helped catapult Tesla to its place as a widely recognised and admired brand across the globe

Netflix

Summary: Netflix is an illustration of how a company could successfully transform itself from a conventional and dotcom-based start-up to a truly digital company. This example gives both hope and direction on how companies from previous generations can transform themselves for the digital era.

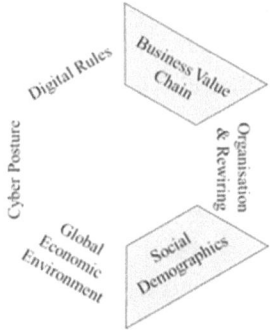

Business Value Chain: Supply Chain, Vendor Management, Big Data management, Cloud, Cognitive, iX (user interaction)

Social Demographics: Population profile

Netflix is a unique company that has transformed itself from a US-centric mail order–based DVD company into a savvy global digital company. The key to its amazing success if that it not only survived the dotcom crash but, while other dotcoms struggled and strove simply to survive, Netflix continuously adapted the digital innovations and trends.

One step at a time in going into the digital direction, Netflix made itself one of the most admired technology companies in the world.

Netflix was one of the early adapters of cloud technology and streaming technology and, at the same time, moved into content production that was well in line with the global demographic trends.

Cloud Strategy

Netflix didn't move to cloud to save costs, but rather to make use of scalability, and also to continue to provide a service in streaming that would be as reliable as what they had successfully managed as a DVD mail-order service. By always working with gold standard and ensuring to make use of the best-of-breed cloud services, Netflix created a strong digital infrastructure.

'Talent at its best'

Netflix has also followed the rule of 'pay them better': the company has paid its staff much higher than the industry norm in terms of salaries. This has always signalled that Netflix values talent.

As a company, it has always had a mission statement, but that statement has changed constantly every year. Overall, its directors believe that they are in a business (of streaming movies over the internet) that's not essential for people.

Workforce Skillsets Beyond CVs

Unlike Yahoo or Google, which have emphasised attracting the personnel with the best CVs and where the leadership often gets involved in tactical items, Reed Hastings has given his team a lot more autonomy and taken the approach that, once the new hire has been with the company for about three months, that's a good enough time to judge whether it is all working out as expected. Making use of its experience with the dotcom crisis, during which the company had to let go over a third of its workforce, Netflix has been better able to adapt to problems where management has to face economic headwinds.

Netflix has cleverly made strong use of the fact that, with the advent of internet, the new generation across the world–NYC, LA, Singapore, Istanbul, London, Paris, Moscow–follows similar content and is often exposed to similar trends, fashions, etc. at about the same time. The rise of global social media sites such as Facebook, YouTube, and Google search have led to more and more uniformity of thoughts and ideas across the urban cultures of the large metropolises the world over.

Furthermore, as more countries adapt to the English language and similar teaching/education standards, the rise of global corporations and global consumer market trends, the global expansion of Hollywood has led to a similar universal acceptance of TV content. As the young generation follows similar global heroes and other marketing blitzes created by global corporations, a rise in similarity of aesthetics and tastes in entertainment has also occurred.

The increased popularity of 60-inch-plus TV screens with exceptional high-definition quality and surround-sound speakers has turned the home into a theatre, sometimes even superior to the real movie theatres. Also, this all is helped by availability of broadband and high-speed internet across the globe. Streaming at high speeds is possible. At the same time, what has gone unnoticed is the use of mobile phones and ultra-thin laptops as receptors to stream movies everywhere. The quality of graphic cards in computers as well as smart devices is of very high resolution. This has meant that we are no longer left yearning for a quality experience outside our homes.

The biggest beneficiary of these changes in technology and global demographic trends, amongst all the media content companies, has been Netflix. By either catapulting on these existing trends or by working in a focused manner to produce clever new content or aspects, it has ensured that it has an edge.

'Millennials will leave organisations unless they have good reasons to stay. So you need to give them something to aspire to.' [36]

Use of Big Data

Netflix has gone as far offering million dollar awards to those who could create better data analytics tools for their searches and other items. Using digital technology to collate the profiles of their clients and providing them with the most appropriate searches has allow Netflix to have the competitive edge as it competes against the giants such as Apple, YouTube and others.

In sum, Netflix managed to forecast the 'conventional fracture' correctly and moved away from DVD mail order business towards

---

[36] https://insight.kellogg.northwestern.edu/article/how-the-us-army-recruits-and-retains-millennials

streaming technology in a timely manner. It continued further through the digital journey by tackling all the key items, which included:
- the vendor/supply chain, where they started creating their own content;
- big data; and
- cloud, by collaborating with the right technology companies early on and being willing to pay for gold standards to keep up with the best of content.

At the same time. Netflix has been able to make use of the superior iX experience created by Samsung, Bose and other companies in making a superior home theatre experience. And the mobility has also been effectively tackled by 4G technology, available globally on HD screen laptops and large-screen mobiles.[37]

Facebook

Summary: Facebook is a truly digital company that over the years has consistently outshone itself. It is a thriving example of a company that shows a lot of the previous strategy views such as 'first mover advantage' aren't always victorious in digital era. To appreciate Facebook fully, many similar themes of existing business models need to be reassessed using the digital spine approach.

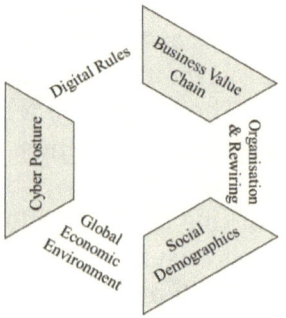

Business Value Chain: Supply Chain, Big Data management, Mobility, Cognitive, iX(user interaction)

Social Demographics: Population profile

Cyber Posture

Facebook is the undeniable leader of the internet, both in social media and in usage. It remains one of the most envied companies today. It has continuously made the case that it's a technology company more than anything else, though most of its critics continuously tag it as an

---

[37] http://www.techrepublic.com/article/5-lessons-it-learned-from-the-netflix-cloud-journey/

advertisement company. It has successfully applied the principle that "if you are not paying, then you are the product."[38]

Facebook has over a billion frequent users. This makes it a very powerful platform to launch any form of product. It has a loyal user base and, furthermore, it has so much personal information at its disposal that it allows companies to be very accurate in terms of their marketing campaigns.

Like Microsoft during its peak with Windows Operating system, Facebook remains a social and media behemoth that now has a substantial influence over all forms of advertising. Along with Google, it dominates the advertisement market across the globe.

Facebooks covers the entire business value chain incredibly well. Analysing Facebook's strengths and advantages across the digital world, one finds that it has many.

Cloud & Mobility

Cloud: Facebook has used the best-of-breed technology and cloud platforms to ensure its systems are always up and running and can manage the huge global traffic.

Mobility: Facebook adapted effectively and very quickly to the mobile technology, even though it started out as a PC-based company.

Superior iX Experience

Even though there were several social media companies launched before Facebook, it remains the most successful and was able to capture everyone's imagination much more quickly.

Facebook took over the mantle from MySpace as the premier social media company. It managed to do this successfully and quickly, owing to some key factors. Looking back at that time in 2010–2011 era, one of the key factors was its laser focus on the interactive experience. Facebook had a much more appealing interactive experience that glued its visitors. The approach and experience was considered so much better that later in 2011 MySpace began almost to imitate Facebook.

Facebook always was a focused social media platform, and it had very few rules for its users. This was quite unlike MySpace, which required anonymous names, imposed restrictions on online games and other uses and almost tried to 'govern' the environment.

---

[38] https://unicornomy.com/how-does-facebook-make-money/

For Facebook and other successful internet companies, the interactive experience is at the heart of its success.

Cognitive

Facebook has effectively launched its own search engine and also a gambit of other software to help keep it abreast of cognitive technologies. Facebook continues to invest in these technologies to experiment in variety of digital ideas to keep abreast in technologies.

Cyber Posture

One of the critical success factors in Facebook remains its ability to maintain a strong cyber posture. It continues to remain at the heart of its successful Digital Spine.

It continues to invest heavily into security upgrades. It's theme is to use a number of independent features, that allows its security to be in the form of several layers. Since its platform is so heavily used it has to use a variety of sophisticated tools to determine trends such as propaganda information and other variety of trends.

It took just three years for FIS (Facebook Immune System) to evolve from basic beginnings into an all-seeing set of algorithms that monitors every photo posted to the network, every status update– indeed, every click made by every one of the 800 million users. There are more than 25 billion of these "read and write actions" every day. At peak activity the system checks 650,000 actions a second.[39]

"It's a big challenge," says Jim Larus, a Microsoft researcher in Redmond, Washington, who studies large networks. The only network bigger, Larus suspects, is the web itself. That makes Facebook's defence system one of the largest in existence.

Despite its efforts it also remains in spotlight and heavily scrutinised by local governments world over owning to its heavy influence over social order and information across the globe.

Social Demographics

Facebook is one of the few companies that have truly captured the mind-set of both the millennials and Gen X.[40] Facebook can take the

---

[39] https://www.newscientist.com/article/dn21095-inside-facebooks-massive-cyber-security-system/

[40] http://panmore.com/facebook-inc-organizational-culture-characteristics-analysis

credit of being one of the few companies that has truly leaped across cultural barriers globally. In a very short time period it has managed to find members across generations but primarily in each country the millennials were the first to leap on it and help it gather critical mass. Its ability to better understand the needs of millennials globally and continuously improving the details, technology and information has kept it critically a favourite hangout site for many.

Snapchat

Summary: Snapchat started with a unique interactive experience that has been an instant success with the millennials. Amongst the demographics and ability to compete against giants like Facebook, its success with the millennials remains quintessential. It now remains to be seen whether Snapchat can dethrone the social media giant Facebook, based on its firm focus on millennials and unique approach to future growth.

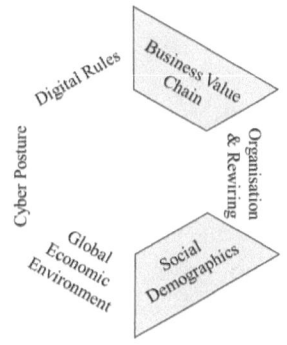

Business Value Chain: Big Data management, Mobility, iX (user interaction)

Social Demographics: Population profile

Snapchat is the trendy new social media platform that has taken the world by storm. Its key competitor Instagram was absorbed by Facebook, making Snapchat in essence now the direct competition of Facebook.

But can Snapchat outgrow Facebook?

Both Snapchat and Facebook have exceptional focus and simple user interface (UI). Both of them have a critical mass, and are well matched across all the key dimensions of the digital spine with the exception of demographics. Snap is distinctly more popular and considered 'cool' amongst the millennials and the even younger generation.

This is a critical issue in the model. If UI and restrictions to environment are not much different, the demographics will determine who will see the expansion. Despite the fact that Facebook has bought

Instagram, its overall brand and environment and users are much older. The fact that teenagers find Facebook full of their parents and other elders makes them more interested in having a somewhat different environment for their hangout, one that feels 'cool' and rebellious. Snapchat fits that bill much better, and hence has the edge.

Social Demographics

'We don't want to be first but want to be first to make it right... Focus and Simplicity.'

— Snapchat's CEO,
on adding new product lines

The success of all new entrants in the digital world has rested above all on some key factors: resolving a problem with focus and simplicity, using an exceptional interactive experience that includes an exceptional user interface and design. In the digital world, from a demographic perspective, the appeal of the interactive experience is at the heart of the solution that attracts primarily millennials.

Amazon (Retail) vs. Walmart

Summary: Amazon and Walmart are two behemoths of the retail industry. One is a textbook example of a company that has done everything right from the classical strategy perspective over the years, and the other is a survivor of the dotcom bust that has turned itself into one of the leading digital companies of the era.

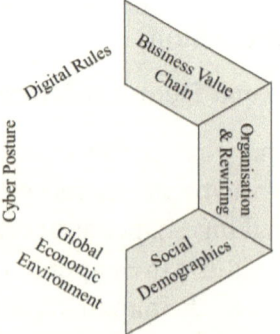

The challenge for Walmart is whether it can change itself swiftly enough to meet the challenges of the digital era, and assess the current landscape to formulate a plan for the future to compete against the likes of Amazon.

At the same time, as Amazon absorbs more conventional business companies, Amazon's challenge is: how does it ensure that it keeps its focus on the right elements so that it remains a leading force in digital era?[41] [42]

Organisation Rewiring

Walmart moved its eCommerce-related teams to Silicon Valley. Specifically, to compete against Amazon and other eCommerce platform and competitors. Walmart has also realized that it's important to hire the right people, create the right culture and attend to other organisational aspects to be able to compete head on against the new generation giants.

It has done so quite effectively and retained a large portion of its market. But despite its best efforts it has been unable to match Amazon, which has a lead over Walmart in spending per customer.

Demographics

Though it might be a small portion of the customer base, Walmart is now making acquisitions in companies that have presence amongst the millennials and have a strong digital brand. This shows that, despite having a lower customer price base, Walmart wants to continue to upgrade and compete as demographics are rapidly changing.

Business Value: Big Data and Supply Chain

Pickup points at Walmart centres will ensure that it's able to gather the right mix of internet and brick-and-mortar business.

Walmart already has a massive database of big data. Also, over several years it has developed with great sophistication an ability to better understand the types of goods that people buy against weather patterns and other such contingencies. Walmart in general has a very good grasp of both its demographic needs and goods and materials to match their needs.

Walmart can easily climb up into the eCommerce domain to continue to service them. Therefore, it will be a fierce competitor. It already has a strong understanding of brick-and-mortar business and

---

[41] https://www.fool.com/investing/2017/02/22/amazon-vs-wal-mart-which-has-the-better-shipping-d.aspx
[42] http://knowledge.wharton.upenn.edu/article/amazon-vs-walmart-one-will-prevail/

has effectively addressed all the logistical issues for transportation, in several instances up to the last mile.

Brand Recognition

Walmart has a well-established brand name across the US for providing best-value-for-money deals in the brick-and-mortar world. It has a very strong and loyal customer base. Though the base has a lower yearly spending level, compared to Amazon and other high-end eCommerce and brick-and-mortar chains, it has the advantage of volume and a head start for close-out and effective end-to-end service.

iX Experience: Key Differentiation between Amazon and Walmart

Along with other items, the key to successful digitisation is the iX experience. This in itself needs to be mastered by Walmart. Amazon and other successful eCommerce sites have mastered this quite well.

Amazon has a much larger depth of online content that's been made available. That almost guarantees that anyone looking for any product will find it on Amazon. Walmart has yet to master this. Its online depth is not comparable to Amazon yet.

Food and grocery retailing is still driven by brick-and-mortar sites. Therefore, how these are merged into existing eCommerce business for both Amazon and Walmart is almost the reverse of how the two companies previously merged brick-and-mortar with eCommerce, with the challenge of attracting higher-spending customers who are more frequent online shoppers.

Apple

Summary: While Apple's story has many facets, we have specifically focused on its successful transformation into a digital company and how during this transformation it has catapulted to the top of the breed of digital companies. In the process it has not only taken over market share from existing corporations in record time but also illustrated how to keep reinventing itself successfully. It thus provides an important example to follow for existing technology companies.

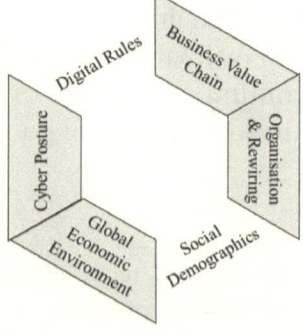

In recent years we have witnessed how Apple has not only captured the mobile market from the likes of Nokia, which crashed from triple-A corporate to bankruptcy, but also taken away the coveted place in having the largest PC base away from Windows OS in USA. Apple continues to grow in both popularity and appeal globally. This brand strength is not simply because of a single competitive advantage; rather, it is a leader in number of digital dimensions. Apple has successfully outmanoeuvred others as the digital environment evolves and matures.

This includes having a product that is considered more stable and secure against its competitors in both PC as well as mobile platforms. It continues to be a leader in its iX appeal both amongst the Gen X and the millennials. By adapting to new trends such as cloud-based technologies (for iTunes amongst others) in a timely manner, and now aggressively entering the cognitive world through Siri and other technologies, Apple continues to remain one of the most cutting-edge companies despite its heft and dominance.

To top it all off, unlike a lot of giants that struggle to take risks while on top, Apple, by hiring selectively from the fashion and design industries, has constantly kept its appeal by staying as the trend setter and successfully rolling out each product and platform with the sharpest focus. It continues to use its cash to try out new products and activities, such as electric cars, and is not afraid of shelving them if they don't meet all its high standards.

People who related to Apple in the past were simply those who were different or artistic or creative. But now the appeal includes those who value price over quality and consider it to be an upmarket product.

Superior Cybersecurity

Apple OS and Apple iOS both remain the leading OS products in today's marketplace. Nowadays we are constantly bombarded with news of how Windows and Android OS have been hit by cyber attacks, but rarely (almost never) do we hear about gaps in the Apple OS systems. It is commonly agreed amongst the cybersecurity experts across the world that Apple OS remains the safest of the products, usually requiring no outside protection.

Apple's approach of having a locked-down OS, better quality control over its applications and other software related products is a huge plus point that its products have over existing open-source and other proprietary technologies. Cybersecurity is typically considered the backbone of the digital products from a protection perspective, and again, like the rest of its features, Apple shows its superiority to its competition by design itself.

Superior iX

Apple has actively hired people from the fashion industry. It has a list of executives who are from the apple industry. It has created one of the most successful store chains across the globe, selling its products directly to consumers. This helped its fan base to come and try new products. Its leading stores, such as Fifth Avenue, have been able to generate additional revenues of hundreds of millions of dollars.

Apple's aesthetics, its design and its interactive experience remain among the best. They have constantly been rated as such by most critics over the decade (or longer). This has ensured that within the digitisation era Apple has been one of the most sought-after brands recognised for superior products, and hence has always commanded a better market value.

Apple has always put an exceptional amount of emphasis on its interactive experience and its aesthetic design, and it's not by accident. Actively hiring leadership and resources to keep working on it has been part of its strategy.

Adapting to Cloud

Apple, despite being best known for its hardware, has also been one of the early adopters of cloud technology. It has had a successful strategy to support its users to backup their music files and other details from both mobile and other devices over to the cloud. Making use of cloud technology has ensured that Apple can secure data and contacts, so that all information is easily transferred in case of loss of equipment.

Brand Recognition

Apple, through its various actions, both with products and by pioneering the approach of having Apple stores to ensure that its customers can better understand and try out new products, has continued to garner brand recognition. Unlike Samsung, which has seen slipups with its phone rollouts and such, Apple has continued to put a tight emphasis on quality and has always been the benchmark in the industry. A lot of companies have come into the competitive second position against its products, but never consistently managed to stay there longer than a few years.

Apple remains one of the most valued brand names across the world. Its brand appeal extends across a wide range of people in society, but primarily it's all those who value its products to be the best and who believe that the high price is well justified by the products' superior quality.

Organisation Rewiring

Apple continues to appeal to the young generation with its strong values and culture. It remains one of the most sought-after companies to work for.

Unique to technology companies, Apple has been appealing to luxury-brand creators and designers amongst its workforce, distinguishing itself from the technology companies of the past that considered the aesthetics as only a last part of the story. Here, Apple embeds aesthetics as a competitive edge, enhancing the overall appeal of the purchase, the marketing and other facets of a truly well-rounded company.

Mastery over Partnership and Vendor Management

Apple has complete insight, and its vendors are almost completely dependent on its orders. Furthermore, the vendors it deals with such as Intel and Foxconn invest heavily, not just to ensure that the products provided are of good quality, but also to meet the acceleration in demand and competitive production lines through continuous R&D.

Global Economic Risk

Apple, like a limited few technology companies, maintains a strong financial position. Unlike many IT companies that have constantly struggled through economic crises, Apple is not only a global corporation but also maintains a strong credit rating enviable to many countries.

With its strong cash flow, Apple has the strength to ensure that it can sustain its market position even during long downturns. Very few technology companies can say this of themselves.

Bitcoin & Other Crypto Currencies

Summary: Is Bitcoin and other crypto currencies simply a digital fad or is this the new reality and part of the digital shift? How do you view the rise and fall of crypto currencies strategically to better value these financial instruments in the new era?

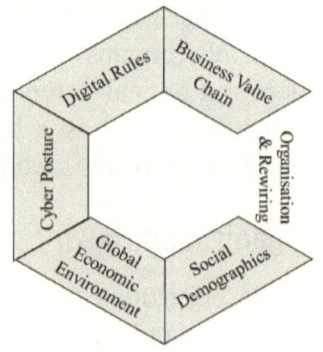

'I think the fact that within the bitcoin universe an algorithm replaces the functions of the government...is actually pretty cool. I am a big fan of Bitcoin'

– Al Gore

Global Economic Contagion Risk/ Credit Risk

Innovation to the rescue?

Rise of bitcoin as a financial instrument of sorts has been because of the crisis and extreme worries that plagued the world in the days and moths after the 2008 Global financial crisis. The crisis exposed the world to a reality where collapse of institutions, countries (in monetary terms such as Iceland) showed the world the vulnerabilities of high finance. One of the core worries amongst the masses globally was the ultimate dependency on country based currencies and dearth of gold available as an alternative.

During the crisis the follies of credit rating agencies, banking and other respectable organisations exposed gaps where for a short while there was extreme suspicion towards any and all instruments controlled by government based institutions.

To help alleviate these pressures and shortfall of a back-up alternative to inflationary currencies a group of individuals developed bitcoin. Bitcoin and early crypto currencies were primarily viewed as a digital innovative option.

Since then it has taken a route of own and now is traded both as a financial instrument or some might claim as a commodity.

Decentralised: During the 2008 crisis one of the core concerns amongst people on the street was that other currencies that can lose value owning to quantitative easing, or inflationary policies of a country this is was considered possible utopian approach to having a global alternative;

Limited availability: The "limited" can often be a misleading word as it simply means that no one can expand the flow of this currency rapidly and cause issues that other country based currencies can cause. The genius lies in the manner the crypto currencies are 'mined' or regenerated that involves a substantial decentralised process. Here also lies one of its most advanced competitive advantages over the existing currency systems that are primarily based on 'trust' of the government institutions. Several of these institutions in hour of crisis can be swayed to behave in strange ways. As witnessed in Germany, Argentina, Brazil, Italy, Venezuela and several African nations amongst others.

Underlying fear of a global contagion like 2008 crisis in developed countries can happen. And the central bankers might unleash extensive quantitative easing.

Digital Rules – Government Regulations & Brand Value

'All it would take would be one terrorist incident in the U.S. funded by bitcoin for the U.S. regulator to much more seriously step in and take action, he said. That's a risk, an unquantifiable risk, bitcoin has that another currency doesn't.'[43]

– Mark Haefele, UBS

Bitcoin is in direct competition with countries' currencies. Local currencies can be controlled by reserve banks to ensure that the local economy is correctly balanced, that usage of currency is restricted to legal use, and that external factors are deterred from causing harm to the country.

Bitcoin by its nature eludes all government regulations. It is therefore banned in most countries, and elsewhere it poses many concerns to those who might want to use it.

---

[43] https://www.bloomberg.com/news/articles/2017-11-17/ubs-shuns-bitcoin-allocations-due-to-threat-of-crypto-crackdown

With the increasing popularity of Bitcoin amongst rogue countries and its use in illegal trade practices, it has often been linked to the 'dark web.'

Retains value: Cryptocurrency valuation is initially set by a process called "Initial Coin Offering" (ICO). It's been observed that some of these have had meteoric rises but also equally dramatic falls.

One of the key reasons for the dramatic fall has been government clampdowns world over. Each time there is a regulatory issue it has a direct impact on the valuation, hence it has remained fairly unstable. But at the same time there seems to be a lot of interest in the currency from various quarters that has continued to keep the momentum moving.

The critics claim that several of the investors are those who are avoiding government taxations or are illicit sources of funds, but at the same time there are also several legitimate investors who believe that this wave will continue. Furthermore, in countries such as Venezuela where there is deep government crisis this has become one of the only sources of creating funds within the country to be able to afford basic goods. Hence bitcoin has taken several difference facets depending on the jurisdiction it's been reviewed from. Overall globally its popularity and notoriety are both increasing. This is leading to a brand value increase as well.

Social Demographics – Population Profile

Bitcoin and crypto currency are more easily accepted by the younger age group. They are more comfortable with digital form of transactions as well innovations. Amongst the older generation there is still the fear that there could be bizarre situations where digital currency could be lost owning to hardware failure or other issues. Younger generation in several developed and developing countries is more accepting to digital economy of all sorts. The generation is only going to expand and take over more and more responsibilities. Therefore, their view of digital currency will play a key role in future developments as well.

Business Value Chain

'Bitcoin is a technological tour de force'

– Bill Gates

Counterfeit currencies are increasing becoming a global menace to manage for paper based currencies. The printing and distribution of currency notes is a huge challenge for countries. The use of electronic version requires payment of commission to banks and other credit card institutions. These all challenges exist with country based currencies.

All of the above challenges are circumvented by bitcoin and other crypto currencies. The currency execution and structuring are based on the Blockchain technology that is far more sophisticated and digital in its nature hence simpler to distribute with minimal risk of being manipulated. Furthermore, with lesser requirements on supply chain such as the banking network amongst other requirements makes its business value chain much more efficient.

Decentralised ledger management using block chain based architecture gives cryptocurrencies a substantial edge over its paper based competitors both in terms of managed and overall efficiency perspective.

Security Posture – Cyber Security

One of the essential pillars of digital age will be how we manage cybersecurity. Nowhere will its presence be more felt than digital finance. With the use of Blockchain technology bitcoin and cryptocurrencies have found themselves in a situation where they are much more advanced in terms of safety and security in comparison to the existing financial instruments and other related items. While paper based currencies, (and derivatives for transactions based on credit cards etc.) are unable to match the sophistication of crypto currencies.

All currencies (and securities based instruments) have a dependency on the country, and global banking infrastructure amongst other details to ensure overall security.

Bit and cryptocurrency have managed to substantially circumvent the need for a 'trust' based system and therefore has challenged the existing banking based distribution system.

Having said that this can all be challenged or put to test as more and more focus comes on cryptocurrencies and if there are hacks or security gaps that expose them.

If any of these are strong gaps not covered quickly it could potentially collapse these currencies. Hence despite the current strength of the technology this fear keeps these currencies highly unstable and there is a substantial worry amongst nations to allow them in the mainstream use of any sorts.

Personal Security vs Public Security

There is a key aspect that needs to be well understood. The bitcoin and cryptocurrency cybersecurity should not be mixed with personal security steps that are required.

"While Blockchain transactions can be used to store data, the primary motivation for bitcoin transactions is the exchange of bitcoin itself; the currency's exchange rate has fluctuated over its short lifetime but has increased in value more than fivefold over the past two years. Each bitcoin transaction includes unique text strings that are associated with the bitcoins being exchanged. Similarly, other Blockchain systems record the possession of assets or shares involved in a transaction. In the bitcoin system, ownership is demonstrated through the use of a private key (a long number generated by an algorithm designed to provide a random and unique output) that is linked to a payment, and despite the value of these keys, like any data, they can be stolen or lost, just like cash. These thefts are not a failure of the security of bitcoin, but of personal security; the thefts are the result of storing a private key insecurely. Some estimates put the value of lost bitcoins at $950 million."[44]

PayPal

Summary: *PayPal is an example of a well-executed fintech strategy and an illustration of how fintechs can quickly transform and challenge the existing financial services sectors and their business niches.*

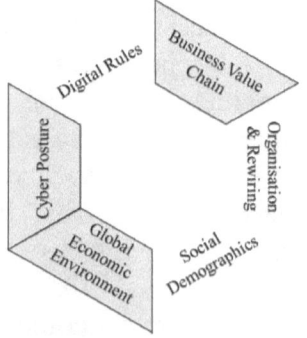

PayPal is a unique digital company that has managed to make a difference in the world of transactions that have long been dominated

---

[44] https://hbr.org/2017/03/how-safe-are-blockchains-it-depends

by the duopoly of Mastercard and Visa. It has done so by revolutionising online payment systems in a way that has given confidence to many who have often worried about online transaction fraud, theft and other cybersecurity issues.

American Express (Amex) lost its market share and appeal over the years to Mastercard and Visa, as they outmanoeuvred Amex globally through savvy marketing and more focused management of the core elements of the transaction business value chain.

PayPal entered the market by introducing an entirely new business model that connected both buyers and sellers with simply the email ID and, in the process, also managed to connect markets globally by handling different currencies as well. By charging a deposit fee and holding the funds for up to 3–4 days, it was also able to make arbitrage on the funds as no one else had access to the funds during that period.

PayPal is one of the early fintechs that have now managed to help a lot of cross-border and other payment issues that the existing duopoly either didn't capture or wasn't interested in.[45] But PayPal's appeal is beyond the business model: it has managed to have a competitive edge in payment world in several dimensions.

PayPal's unique selling point to users has been its ability to safe guard consumer credit card details and consumer rights on the authenticity of the merchant services. This innovative approach to help consumer's transact online without concerns of their credit card information getting hacked or misused has been a key selling point.

Supply Chain

PayPal, through its merger of companies during its initial days, successfully managed to sign up with eBay. This has since ensured it has a substantially large and established user base.

Vendor Partnership

With the establishment of eBay and its initial success, it has since managed to become the mode of payment choice for online users across the world who had been worried about sharing their data, identity and bank details over the internet. With fraud as the primary concern, PayPal has successfully reduced this and also built confidence amongst

---

[45] https://unicornomy.com/how-does-paypal-make-money-business-model/

its army of users. Further, PayPal has allowed the seller base to increase by allowing transactions to take place simply by the use of emails rather than requirement of bank accounts.

Cyber Security Posture

Cybersecurity innovations used by PayPal are at the heart of its consumer success. One of the most daunting task faced by consumers is to use the credit card details online. The number of cases of credit card information getting hacked, misused, has increased over the years. PayPal through its unique ability to facilitate the payment between the consumer and merchant by keeping the privacy and consumer rights intact has been an instant success. This feature introduced by PayPal at a global scale has helped support confidence in online transaction amongst consumers. PayPal has given an opportunity to smaller enterprises to trade online as consumers wouldn't have easily entrusted them with their credit card details. This has cybersecurity solution is at the heart of PayPal's success amongst online consumers world over.

Credit Risk

First with the heft of its backers and later through sheer size, PayPal has very quickly established itself as an entity of credible worthiness. This is critical in the world of banking and online payment, when one is dealing with a brand that has no recognition and could be tainted or have credit risk attached to it. It remains a separate entity rather than part of any bank; therefore, it remained unscathed during the banking crisis of 2008.

WeWork

Summary: *Digital organisations will rotate around a new approach to organisation, culture of work and this is most easily identified by the office space set up and how that helps relate to the new-age interaction experience. WeWork has successfully identified this subtle change and risen an organisation from the ashes of 2008 property collapse that marked the end of easy credit cycle and age old work organisation culture. Along with all this comes WeWork's ability to manage data*

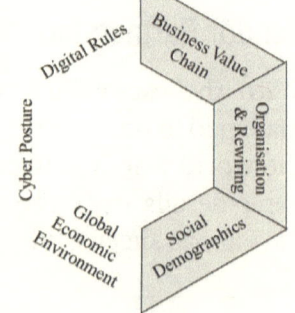

to accurately understand minute details such as: heat, sound travel in decibels and similar details that impact the focus of the worker/employee. With a mix of digital skills it has created a superior interactive floor space experience and transformed the office culture across continents.

Superior Interactive Experience

WeWork has a new-age office setup, focusing on aesthetics and details in line with millennial expectations, an area where they can hang out and meet similar people with ideas and values and cross-pollinate on business thoughts. But there is more to it than just aesthetics: many of the floor space activities are matched with data available from existing floor spaces and their impact on work and culture.

The company has given specifically a lot of emphasis on two key items: light and large common spaces. The correct balance of these two has helped it create vibrant co-working atmosphere.

Hence, many would argue WeWork might even be seen as a technology company rather than simply a floor space management company.[46]

Mobility

WeWork has expanded rapidly, not only across North America but also in Europe and Asia. The concept of co-working has caught up with many in the younger generation. The sites with the flexibility of the charging model are both appealing and efficient for the young entrepreneur. WeWork has simply followed, as technology has transformed the employee's worksite from fixed desk to mobile. Therefore, as this concept has expanded outside North America, it continues to follow the mobility path.

Social Demographics

WeWork and similar co-working sites have embraced the open office space concept, mixed with an ambience that's made of a relaxing atmosphere, infused water to drink, and a 'latte culture.' These businesses cater to millennials interested in experimenting with new ideas, seeing the world and mixing with similar-thinking people across

---

[46] http://www.businessinsider.sg/weworks-secret-weapon-will-be-data-2016-5/

their journeys. For these digital nomadic travellers the co-working sites dotted across the globe are quite useful and make sense.

Organisation Rewiring

In terms of the workforce interaction experience, people both working for the company and its clients have a high opinion of the working experience. WeWork has created a superior physical working experience both for its clients and its own workforce. It has therefore been able to attract the millennials and the sophisticated engineers to work for it. This also plays a key role in the setup of the overall brand image of the company, as many of these folks would either rate their experience online or give feedback to friends and others about it.

New Markets

'Times and conditions change so rapidly that we must constantly aim for the future.'

– Walt Disney

New competitors in most industry verticals are able to better harness the Blue Ocean Strategy–based markets or simply new markets that were previously unavailable in the existing environment.

People may find it more useful to use the credit points given by car sharing apps than those offered by banks. These car sharing apps will soon have an even larger trove of digital knowledge of where people go for better deals on restaurants and shops in the vicinity. This is just one example of how digital activities are overcoming the barriers that in previous years guarded the industries.

New Partnerships

As the companies jump over the barriers, old companies with existing market shares will have to face the threats in new and rapid ways. Many of them may consider partnerships or acquisitions. This will mean a clash of cultures in instances where both the companies are of large sizes, as neither can absorb the other.

The dotcom era is well documented. The clash of cultures of AOL and Time Warner during their merger is well known.[47] Both companies had the best of intentions to help rise rapidly to gain market share as well as be a technology behemoth, but the management clashes ensured the merger would be a failure. There is a strong possibility that such issues can repeat themselves, hence the organisation and rewiring activities will have to play a strong role in execution strategies and the details within them. A successful

---

[47] https://www.newyorker.com/magazine/2003/01/27/the-culture-excuse

execution strategy is not only about the external activities but also how well the management has handled the internal issues. Workforce skillsets of organisations will need to be better aligned so that everyone can be rewarded.

'In the end, Jerry Levin, Bob Pittman, and Steve Case didn't fall victim to any conflict between the arrogance of AOL and the fustiness of Time Warner. They fell victim to history, by betting on an AOL-centric future that hasn't materialized. (It may someday, but for their purposes someday is too late.) In the years after the merger was announced, the Internet bubble burst, the Net advertising market dried up, AOL's subscriber growth slowed to almost nothing, its profits fell by a billion dollars, and millions of people started using broadband, where AOL scarcely has a toehold. Those facts would have doomed Case and Levin even if they had figured out how to get all their employees singing the same tune. Sure, culture makes a difference, but, as Tom Peters, who helped popularize the idea, has said, "The corporate-culture thing has been so simplified, cheapened, bastardized." The synergy gurus at AOL Time Warner have now taken their leave. Perhaps the culture gurus will follow suit.

In 2017, AOL announced it is sun-setting its famous AOL messenger service, as it no longer has a large enough user base.

Better Efficiency and Matching Quality

'Necessity is not an established fact but an interpretation.'

– Friedrich Nietzsche

Summary: *Digital companies have replaced several of the existing conventional notions of what it means to launch a successful business value chain. In previous years, one needed to own a certain amount of physical inventory across a variety of industries, but that has all been replaced by a very efficient pay-as-you-go model in many of those verticals, coupled with efficient payment and information systems. All these together have helped create an entirely new marketplace for new start-ups and young entrepreneurs. The barriers that existed previously and were preached in classical business models as a core piece of strategy have now evaporated.*

Digital companies have been able to offer similar quality (or in some instances even better) at a fraction of the original price. Further, the new-age companies are almost always very asset-light. This has meant that the majority of their spending is driven towards marketing or connecting with the value chain using electronic methods.

Culture and Fresh Organisation

These companies in most instances are fresh, and hence in the people environment the culture is much more vibrant.[48] They are not inhibited by existing bureaucracies or fiefdoms that often come into existence in organisations that are over a decade old and have structured themselves as per the previous economic requirements. In the older businesses there are often more inefficiencies, gaps and other organisational issues that higher management is unable to tackle. This plays directly into the hands of new competitors. They are much nimbler and possess more of the backing and depth of shrewd venture capital industry experience to know how to ensure sophisticated, best-of-breed leadership. Most of these organisations are private or have recently moved into the limited public sector, and therefore are able to hire strong, young and aggressive talent coupled with new knowledge and understanding from universities.

Superior iX Experience

All new-age internet companies that have become behemoths (Facebook, Amazon, Netflix, etc.) have in common that they have the most superior iX experience in their domains. The website and overall iX experience is exceptionally focused and kept sleek. In the iX experience of these applications and sites, there is no doubt in what's expected from the user and the purpose. This ensures that, even if they have competitors, they are have outdone them.

This also remains at the heart of the entire digital experience and branding. Brand is built primarily around the interactive experience, and other aspects may or may not be included in the overall scheme of dimensions.

---

[48] http://www.mckinsey.com/business-functions/digital-mckinsey/our-insights/culture-for-a-digital-age

Adapting Visions and Mission Statements to Market Changes

The Netflix CEO has mentioned repeatedly that he thinks the mission statement is key, though he has realised he has to change it every year, which reflects that he has found himself not fighting but adapting to repeatedly moving market conditions.

Facebook has a laser focus on social media. Its competitor from earlier days, which tried to fight the market conditions and made efforts to control the environment rather than adapting to changing conditions and customer needs, fell by the wayside. This phenomenon of adaptability is both useful and essential in the digital era, that is, rapidly changing, and its new forms require proactive changes in the interactive experience, as client needs have to be met. At the heart of it all remains that the iX experience must remain superior and must always match precisely with its clients' needs.

Social Demographics

Almost definitely, with time and with the rise of millennials in the workforce and the extensive use of mobility devices, acceptance amongst the young generation is almost always key for the rise of the companies. Indeed, the companies profiled here all have a large appeal amongst the millennials.

Mobility

'Best teachers are those who tell where to look, but don't tell you what to see.'

– Alexandra K. Trenfor

Summary: Our use of interaction has completely transformed in the past decade with the advent of smartphones and the increasing speed of wireless, chips and an ever more attractive user experience. Furthermore, amongst the millennials and the working population that's always on the move, this has turned into an essential part of their daily life, in some instances even more than their wallet.

With the rise of mobile devices, all the new companies inevitably had to adapt their usage for a population that is always on the move.

This has meant continuously changing the interactive experience, amongst other details, to adapt to mobile technology.

Misconception of Business-to-Business Enterprise

'Why is it so difficult for established companies to pull off the new growth that business model innovation can bring? Here's why: They don't understand their current business model well enough to know if it would suit a new opportunity or hinder it, and they don't know how to build a new model when they need it.'[49]

– Mark W. Johnson et al. 2008

The biggest misconception of so many large business-to-business enterprises is that, as long as they can target needs of their existing clients, they are meeting their Client needs and from business perspective well covered. Most large businesses feel that the needs of large enterprises are congruent with the more mature marketplace and that they should not have to consider the models profiled here, as their needs are different.

History shows that many large companies that see erosion in the small-enterprise businesses often see their large-enterprise clients get eroded as well. Furthermore, a lot of the small and micro companies are led by young entrepreneurs who again fall in the demographics of millennials or, if in early 30s, will work at the pace of the millennials to make a difference. Companies that are focused on this group will see revenues, profits and their fates turn in a much more favourable direction.

It has been observed that the current revolution in digitisation was initiated first in in the business-to-consumer market. A lot of companies that are primarily focused on the consumer market are ahead in terms of innovation in the digital sphere. Therefore, many of the new-generation entrepreneurs, by focusing on small SMEs that are sometimes closer to consumer markets, are able to catch on to trends better.

Let us take the example of Amazon Cloud. This product innovation has stayed in existence because of the availability of extra capacity caused when it endeavoured to meet the needs of the holiday season

---

[49] https://www.innosight.com/insight/reinventing-your-business-model/

demand. The initial buyers for a long time were the small – and medium-scale business as well as consumer buyers, while the larger players such as IBM kept waiting for the market to mature and focused on only the business-to-business markets of their larger customers. During this delay, Amazon managed a head start over several technology giants. As it matured, it was able to work on a variety of solutions and offerings and to attract better talent to start this division, almost from the ground up, while the existing technology companies, despite having strong talent, never created the right environment to capture this market. Furthermore, with lack of experience in the sales cycle, they kept stumbling as they tried to find the right mix with the organisations. Several, such as IBM and Microsoft, lost years in this process and now are fighting for business at a much lower profit margin and trying to make up for that lost time.

As long as the companies qualify on the key digital aspects of the model and at the same time are focusing on these very small enterprises that are catering to the shifting marketplace and generational needs, we are going to see the biggest winners (and some losers of lost opportunities as well!).

Let us take the example of INTUIT, which is one such company that is making this difference through its software. By focusing more and more on the needs of small enterprises and even the Uber-based freelancers who are growing in number, it will see a rise in its software and demand. As it adds value along with artificial intelligences and cognitive tools, there is a greater probability of their doing a better job for the future in AI, in contrast with solutions which are so overly focused only on the large enterprises that often falter or are too slow to implement anything in a meaningful manner. INTUIT, with its fast turnaround and feedback cycle, will be able to reach a large critical mass as well as produce nimbler and more cost-effective AI tools for the coming decade.

Lessons from the Dotcom Bubble and Other Market Madness in Financial History

We have specifically noted in the model there is a mention of the global economic environment. In the recent years the market to borrow funds both for start-ups and for large businesses has been fairly benign. This is owing to a condition of excessive 'quantitative easing.' But this support won't last forever. Furthermore, many might begin to forget, but the dotcom crash followed by the credit crisis led to wider global contagions and destroyed a number of fledgling and established businesses. Eras of easy money come and go. Each time there is euphoria, it is likely to be followed by a crash, and in each crash many businesses that think they're doing everything right fail as well. Therefore, it is important that, no matter how the business strategy is viewed there needs to be financial sense that goes with it. Understanding the credit worthiness of a business and the current economic cycle, to better gauge the variables related to funding, is required to survive crisis.

Netflix and Amazon are both examples of companies that survived the dotcom bubble. Netflix went through a financial crunch situation where it had to lay off many employees for several consecutive months. But unlike so many others during that era, it was able to navigate across. This is critical for digital-era companies as well. Sometimes the business model might be completely relevant, but the given economic environment conditions can be so extreme as to call for special measures.

In such situation, there are five key questions to be asked:
1. What is the credit rating per the financial institutions of both the business and the industry?
2. What is the risk of a global economic contagion and its impact on the business?
3. Can the business survive or even benefit from a contagion scenario?
4. Would a global economic contagion provide more weightage to the digital model or instead erode its importance?
5. In extreme situations, would people flock to this business model vs. the existing conventional options?

Digital Momentum to Success: Seven Elements

'Study the past if you would divine the future'

– Confucius

Summary: *What are the list of questions that businesses need to ask to gauge their preparedness in digital business strategy and competition? Following is a list of key questions that will help clarify the momentum for success.*

These questions are in context of the industry; therefore, responses should be benchmarked accordingly:

Question 1: CLIENTS: Are your millennial clients increasing? If the company is business-to-business, at what rate are small-scale companies managed by millennials in your clientele increasing in number?

Question 2: BRAND: What is the brand recognition amongst millennials?

Question 3: TRAININGS/ SKILLS: How many new digitally trained/ skilled employees does the organisation have in ratio terms? For instance, how many data scientists to employees, new-skill trained people vs those with the older skillsets? By 'new skill' is meant, if the industry requires robotics-based factories, how many people in the group are trained to handle the robots or have working knowledge or experience related to the robotic environment?

Question 4: iX EXPERIENCE: How is the interface experience of the company, both internal and external, rated against the competition? Is it within one to three of the best? (The rest does not matter.)

Question 5: BUSINESS VALUE CHAIN: Is the entire business value chain digitised? There is a difference between automation and the digital value chain; whereabouts is the organisation in terms of this transformation?

Question 6: GOVERNMENT REGULATIONS: What is the impact of government regulations on the future business? Are the regulations clarified, or are they still being debated?

Question 7: CYBERSECURITY: When was the last time there was an end-to-end cybersecurity assessment of IT and other operations carried out? Is the cybersecurity risk log managed by the CFO with real dollar figures and reserves?

The execution of digital spine programmes usually starts with design thinking workshops in which various skills are represented for fully covering the digital spine. The seven elements may serve as a basis to check against completeness. Prototyping in an initial stage usually leads to best results, as this allows interactive experience which may be challenged easily by the users of business lines. This provides fast feedback, and allows possibilities to adjust almost on the spot.

Most businesses today are still not fully comfortable with this style of working. Companies should rely on new adequate execution strategies.[50]

Societal Change Owing to Digitisation

As in previous industrial revolutions, there will be dramatic advancement in production as well as a substantial shift in skillsets, and thus job losses amongst those ill-equipped to adapt to this change. In this cycle, this all will cause the middle class fabric to be substantially eroded.

Furthermore, the existing large corporations and businesses will be severely impacted, as they will need to adapt to changes in technology. In some instances, they will suffer losses caused by a new breed of competitors (purely digital in nature); in others, those left behind will be those that are in self-denial and haven't adapted to changes in time. In all instances, there will directly and indirectly lead to substantial financial write-offs and loss of employment. The way of life of lifelong employees will be put to severe tests.

Learn to Work with Millennials

Digitisation will change the employment landscape. Millennials (the younger generations) are best suited for this new technology change.

Millennials will soon start to take over ownership and management of most of the future businesses. Millennials will play a pivotal role in decision-making of companies that will succeed or fail. In the approach to much of the decision-making process, the expectations will be quite different from existing management styles and approaches. Some of this scenario is quite normal with change of generations, but it will be a painful change for many who have grown accustomed to an existing style. The real surprise will be the speed and momentum with which the change of hands may occur across organisations and industries.

Col Robert Carr, US Army Fellow has written the subject. One his articles mentions, 'You don't want a bunch of bobbleheads who can't think for themselves, but you do want to provide discipline and structure to the way that millennials present new ideas,' Carr explains

---

[50] https://hbr.org/sponsored/2017/03/how-organizations-can-thrive-in-the-digital-economy

with reference to how the U.S. Army recruits and retains millennials.[51] 'This gives the military a framework to honour the past, capitalize on the moment, and posture for the future.'

Expectations of Millennials

"Millennials, instead of a danger, are really a reflection of the society in which they grew up in, and in which all of us now live."

– Crystal Kadakia

Since millennials will soon account for the largest work force across the globe, as well as being the next generation of the human mankind, it's important to understand their values and expectations better. This will have a large impact on not only the working of the company but also how it is perceived and valued. 'Millennials will leave organisations unless they have good reasons to stay. So you need to give them something to aspire to,' Carr adds.[52]

Millennials follow new paradigms:
1. 'Career not a job.'
2. Role of social media.
3. Importance of relationships in the working environment.
4. Importance of creating a fun work environment.
5. Sharing/collaboration rather than secrecy with information.
6. 'We are not climbing the ladder; we are circumventing it.'
7. 'We've learnt from our parents' mistakes.'

These paradigms are a summary from various sources listed below.
a. Mallory Schlossberg, "The surprising things millennials love – and hate," Business Insider 2015;

http://www.businessinsider.sg/what-retailers-should-know-millennials-love-and-hate-2015-9/?r=US&IR=T
b. Merge Gupta Sunderji, "Four things millennials hate about you," The Globe and Mail 2014:

https://beta.theglobeandmail.com/report-on-business/careers/leadership-lab/four-things-millennials-hate-about-you/article17721456/?ref=http://www.theglobeandmail.com&

---

[51] https://insight.kellogg.northwestern.edu/article/how-the-us-army-recruits-and-retains-millennials
[52] https://insight.kellogg.northwestern.edu/article/how-the-us-army-recruits-and-retains-millennials

c. The Deloitte Millennial Survey 2017

   https://www2.deloitte.com/global/en/pages/about-deloitte/articles/millennialsurvey.html
d. Lauren Martin, "50 Things About Millennials That Make Corporate America Sh*t Its Pants," Elite Daily 2014;

   http://elitedaily.com/life/50-things-millennials-make-corporate-america-uncomfortable/758330/
e. Sharon Terlep, "Millennials, as Seen by Corporate America," Wall Street Journal 2017;

   https://graphics.wsj.com/glider/millennials-c671d444–6267–4e9b-ba6b-384a5b2fdb03
f. Samuel Tsien, "Give millennials the flexibility they need to explore and grow," LinkedIn 2017;

   https://www.linkedin.com/pulse/give-millennials-flexibility-need-explore-grow-samuel-tsien

Ageism Will Become More Evident

'The saddest aspect of life is that science gathers knowledge faster that society gathers wisdom.'

– Isaac Asimov

Summary: Ageism is the darker side of reality in Silicon Valley and computer software engineering the world over. People above the age of 35 years will find it much hard to find a job, and those over 40 may find themselves completely excluded from future projects.

One of the trends noted in Silicon Valley has been how hard it is becoming to find employment beyond the age of 30. Often, as we have seen, trends that start in Silicon Valley are followed across other technologically advanced countries. This trend reflects the fact that digital technology is quite different from existing technology and requires skillsets that are quite new and that the culture and approach to work are going to be different as well.

A recent article in USA Today reported that those over age 40 found themselves over the hill when looking for a tech job.[53] A Financial

---

[53] https://www.usatoday.com/story/tech/columnist/2017/08/04/ageism-forcing-many-look-outside-silicon-valley-but-tech-hubs-offer-little-respite/479468001/

Times article noted the story of a 62-year-old man who, despite years of experience with Hewlett-Packard, Sun Microsystems and Cisco, was losing out on jobs to people 'earlier in their career.'[54] A woman who was hired at Google at 52 described on Wired the issues older tech employees face with career development, lack of mentoring programs and socializing — although she noted she survived 'karaoke, rock climbing and a folkloric overnight ski trip.'[55] [56]

At the same time, many people in long-term employment may see loss of employment and no new positions available, as the skillsets required will be such that decades of experience, absent the skills created in the last two or three years, may look meaningless on the CV. At the turn of the 20th century (during the previous industrial revolution), a bullock cart driver might have years of experience driving a bullock cart, but that was a different driving skillset than a locomotive driver. Many of us have grown up learning to drive a car in the IC engine era, some even with manual gear shifts. In the new age of Tesla, IC engine and gears may soon be obsolete and, with driverless capability, make the previous generation's skillset meaningless.

Some of these changes will be subtle and others quite evident, but in either case they will pervasively change our way of life and the meaning of the skillsets we value.

End of the Middle Class

'It was the labor movement that helped secure so much of what we take for granted today. The 40-hour work week, the minimum wage, family leave, health insurance, Social Security, Medicare, retirement plans. The cornerstones of the middle-class security all bear the union label.'

– Barack Obama

Summary: *A class that was created at the end of World War II owing to stability of employment and the rise of large enterprises and stable developed countries faces a challenge of survival.*

---

[54] https://www.ft.com/content/d54b6fb4-624c-11e7-91a7-502f7ee26895
[55] https://www.wired.com/story/surviving-as-an-old-in-the-tech-world/;
[56] https://www.cnbc.com/2017/09/18/even-35-year-olds-may-feel-ageism-in-tech-google-amazon-engineers.html?recirc=taboolainternal

Like the changes in previous industrial revolutions, there will be substantial changes in society caused by loss of stable employment. During this industrial cycle, this all will lead to the erosion of the middle-class fabric. Furthermore, the existing large corporations and businesses will be severely impacted. In some instances it is owing to losses caused by the new breed of competitors that are purely digital in nature; in others, those that are left behind are in self-denial and haven't adapted to changes in time. This will lead to substantial write-offs and loss of employment, and hence the savings of employees will be put to severe tests. This all will lead to instability of pensions, long-term saving plans and other such schemes that require employees to contribute over a longer period. As in this new era, for at least the next decade as the shift marches across industries and countries, there will be fewer stable employment positions available.

End of Pension Funds

'However my parents – both of whom came from impoverished backgrounds and neither of whom had been to college, took the view that my overactive imagination was an amusing quirk that would never pay a mortgage or secure a pension.'

– J.K. Rowling

Summary: One of the key impacts of this revolution will be instability in employment and hence savings of all sorts. Pensions and similar large-scale savings will come under sharp stresses, and in several countries disappear.

With the end of stable employment will follow the end of long-term savings plans, as pensions are stashed in blue chips, they will hold lesser cash reserves for employee pensions. A class of people and a class of cash reserve that started at the end of Second World War will come to an end.

In many large corporations during the era of the previous dotcom bubble burst, followed by the financial crisis of 2008, pension schemes were redefined. They changed from defined-benefit schemes to defined-contribution schemes. This, in a nutshell, means that employees are no longer guaranteed a defined sum of money during their retirement. Instead, they have to work with the challenges of the markets at the time of their retirement that will define how much is available for the rest of their days.

Going forward, we will see a substantial erosion of all sorts of pension schemes. As all of these schemes mentioned are primarily based on a pyramid structure, they count on those coming into the labour force to be more numerous than the previous generation and thus better equipped to sustain the burden of funding the greying population. But in the current era, the new labour force may not hold long-term employment; the millennial workforce will be lesser in number than greying population or, having lost out in the technology battles, unable to sustain burdens of heavy pension schemes.

All these and other reasons mean that the system of pensions, as defined at the end of World War II and continuing until recently, may soon be a phenomenon of the past. This would possibly be the single largest loss and change impacting employment patterns for the future. With this kind of insecurity, people will revisit the types of degrees and employment they pursue, and also which towns and cities they would want to settle in for the future.

As quoted by The Guardian Newspaper UK in a detailed pension related article, 'Those most exposed to the great pension shortfall are not those just entering the workforce, most of whom presume they will work until their 70s and will receive limited support from the state. Those most at risk of enduring a penny pinching older age are those in their 40s and 50s who grew up assuming that the pensions system their parents enjoyed – generous income, retirement in their mid-60s – was the norm.'[57]

End of Global Trade and WTO?

Summary: As some countries fall behind in generating employment opportunities, further there are stresses in existing trade imbalances, there will be a rise both populist movements and other strains that will lead several leaders to question existing deals, and trade quotas.

As employment drops dramatically across the globe, owing first to automation of industries and later to digitisation, it will lead to political crises. With extreme efficiency across industries and

---

[57] https://www.theguardian.com/membership/2017/jan/23/saving-retirement-pension-generation-old-age

changes in manufacturing platforms in Industry 4.0, there will be new winners and losers across the globe. This means that the industries and countries that once commanded competitive advantages under past conditions may now be at the losing end. When Finland suffered the loss of Nokia, its means of a lead in technological competitiveness, it involved the downfall not only of the large corporation but also of many smaller-scale companies, affecting families and communities that were heavily dependent on its success. We will be seeing such losses on a much wider scale across the globe in the coming two decades.

Changes in technology and hence employment patterns will in turn lead to substantial changes in societies and hence cause ripple effects across the political landscape. Many will question the need for global trade agreements, and will be critical of those leaders who are unable to give them adequate protection against the extreme loss in employment and trade imbalances.

The World Trade Organization (WTO) has been at the centre of most of the global trade agreements; these will now go through severe stresses and strains. Also, other global organisations and bilateral trade agreements might be reassessed as all nations try various approaches to protect employment opportunities within their boundaries.

Acceleration of Space Exploration

Summary: The world is not enough, as technology and economies will compete for more share of resources, markets and growth they will begin to look beyond earth...

'I would like to die on Mars. Just not on impact.'

– Elon Musk

As opportunities on Earth look limited (initially at least), there will be a call to expand for space exploration. With the availability of sophisticated cognitive tools, they will assist in a variety of space missions. Some could be collaborative with robots; others that are more treacherous or scouting-related would require many more of the automated voyager-style missions, but much more sophisticated and advanced that what we have witnessed so far.

As countries like India manage to launch satellite missions for the same price as making a space-themed Hollywood movie would cost, it shows there is much room to cut down on costs and expenses currently projected by the likes of NASA. Countries like India are not only getting more sophisticated but are finding innovative ways to cut costs as well, and to collaborate globally to manage end-to-end supplies and commercially viable models.

With increase in commercial companies getting involved, increasing better robotics tools (owning to AI technology) and other digital improvements, we will witness space exploration vehicles get ever more sophisticated and efficient. Sci-fi movies such as Star Wars continue to enthral imaginations and several aspects are now looking feasible as digital companies and their business models are becoming ever more successful and getting venture funding.

Government-Led Initiatives and Expansion of Public Sector Role

Summary: How does the government react to the changes in society as some will be well paid while others with no hope of employment? How will the government react to change business landscape as several large enterprises might not survive hence there will be a substantial loss of tax collection and other forms revenue for public sector funding?

As we know that everyone can't be highly competent technically, or even fortunate enough to find a place in a technology sector owing to limited opportunities, there will be a need to explore other avenues to sustain oneself. As employment in private sectors dries up, there will be added pressure on every government to create new jobs to help provide some form of employment to its citizens. Look no further and see the developing countries that are facing problems with employment and how the governments have tried to tackle these issues. These include:
- larger military and paramilitary forces and roles;
- larger pools of administrative roles in the public sector; and
- education and social service–related roles.

The public sector will become an important source of employment; hence, there will be much more focus on ensuring that the masses have some options and avenues available.

Exploring New Avenues in Other Roles in Nature

With the availability of more sophisticated technology, there will be added pressure for new generations to find jobs that previously were shunned in order to stay within the urban boundaries. More and more of the younger generation may be willing to explore work situations that were previously considered far more isolated in nature. We may see a new hybrid kind of jobs emerge that will require explorations, as well activities over longer periods outside of urban areas.

Conclusion

'Once a decision was made I did not worry about it afterwards.'

– Harry S. Truman

We hope this book is able to provide you with answers to several of the questions that have bewildered many with regards to the changes of the new-age industrial revolution.

We specifically use the term 'industrial revolution' not only because of the scale of change, but also because it is like a global revolution where many preconceived views held for decades (if not for almost a century!) will come to an end. With such massive changes in the forefront it is important that, unlike with previous changes, everyone during this industrial revolution is better prepared with the information at hand. People must have a better understanding of the distinction between the successful and failing companies in the digitisation era. In this era where information flows more rapidly, and more and more people across the world have access to it almost instantaneously, we hope these details are better harvested by as many as possible.

The model gives an overview across a variety of industries, and a common theme from which to dive deep into various ideas and thoughts with regards to what needs to be done per business.

The model helps to provide framework and reduce the 'art' and intuitive nature by which several of the decisions are being taken to adapt to the digital age. We hope by using the framework for brainstorming and putting in details across the various topics it helps give better clarity and vision for taking better directional decisions.

This book gives insights to both entrepreneurs and those who are part of failing enterprises that need to transition. It seeks to address the core questions to ask, to better understand the changing landscape.

About the Authors

Vikram Kalkat is a business development executive who specialises in launching new technologies. Vikram has several years of experience as a strategy and digital transformation consultant, advising multinationals across the globe. Over the years he has helped clients across Europe, North America and Asia address the hard business and directional issues. He is a recognised speaker on cybersecurity issues. Prior to this book, he has written on new approaches to financial credit risk, and strategy modelling amongst other initiatives.

Reto Gruenenfelder is the founder and owner of crITadvisory Pte. Ltd., a digital transformation advisory boutique in Singapore. Previously he was with IBM as Vice President & Distinguished Engineer, covering its financial services clients across the globe. Reto has advised clients on initiatives related to Enterprise Architecture, Blockchain and Artificial Intelligence amongst other leading technology aspects. He has worked with start-ups to help support upcoming digital ecosystems.

www.ingramcontent.com/pod-product-compliance
Lightning Source LLC
Chambersburg PA
CBHW030906180526
45163CB00004B/1732